W9-CCI-484

ST PHILIP NERI

DILECTUS DEO ET HOMINIBUS

SAINT PHILIP NERI

*(From an engraving in the second edition of the life of the Saint
by Domenico Sonzonio, published at Padua in 1733)*

ST PHILIP NERI

Apostle of Rome and Founder of the Congregation of the Oratory

BY

V. J. MATTHEWS
Priest of the London Oratory

*"Therefore, whilst we have time, let us
work good to all men, but especially to those
who are of the household of the faith."*
—Galatians 6:10

TAN BOOKS AND PUBLISHERS, INC.
Rockford, Illinois 61105

Cum licentia Visitatoris Apostolici

NIHIL OBSTAT:

EDUARDUS MAHONEY, S.Th.D.,
Censor deputatus.

IMPRIMATUR:

✠ JOSEPH BUTT,
Vicarius generalis.

WESTMONASTERII,
die 19a Julii, 1934.

First published in 1934 by Burns Oates & Washbourne Ltd., London. Rights purchased from the London Oratory in 1984 by TAN Books and Publishers, Inc. Reprinted by TAN Books and Publishers, Inc. in 1984.

Copyright © 1984 by TAN Books and Publishers, Inc.

Library of Congress Catalog Card No.: 84-50406

ISBN: 0-89555-237-X

All rights reserved. No part of this book may be reproduced or transmitted in any form or by any means, electronic or mechanical, including photocopying, recording, or by any information storage or retrieval system without permission in writing from TAN Books and Publishers, Inc.

Printed and bound in the United States of America.

TAN BOOKS AND PUBLISHERS, INC.
P.O. Box 424
Rockford, Illinois 61105

1934

REVERENDISSIMO ET CARISSIMO

PATRI

JOSEPH M. TORRENT I LLOVERAS

PRESBYTERO CONGREGATIONIS BARCINONENSIS

ORATORII SANCTI PHILIPPI NERII

PRO PIGNORE CARITATIS ILLIUS QUAE

INTER FILIOS DIVERSOS EIUSDEM BEATI PATRIS

VINCULUM PRAESTAT UNICUM

OPUSCULUM HOC DEDICAT

CONGREGATIONIS LONDINENSIS

PRESBYTER

CONTENTS

PUBLISHER'S PREFACE

St. Philip Neri (1515-1595) lived in one of the most eventful centuries in the history of the Church: the time of the Protestant Revolt, the Council of Trent (1545-1563), and the Catholic Counter-Reformation. Although the Church was then suffering from great laxity among both clergy and lay people, the 16th century was also the "Century of the Saints," to use St. Robert Bellarmine's apt expression. St. Philip was a contemporary of numerous canonized saints, including St. Teresa of Avila, St. John of the Cross, and St. Francis Xavier, and he knew personally St. Ignatius Loyola and St. Charles Borromeo.

Yet when we read the life of St. Philip Neri, we find very little reference to the momentous events taking place in the Church as a whole. Unlike many of the great saints of that era, St. Philip found that his vocation was to a single city. At the beginning of the 16th century, the religious situation in Rome was corrupt and lukewarm, and the people lived in a state of spiritual malaise. St. Philip's mission was to convert and sanctify innumerable souls in Rome by preaching in the marketplaces, hearing confessions, directing souls, caring for the sick in the primitive hospitals of the day, ministering to needy pilgrims, and performing miracles, as well as by searching out wayward souls who did not recognize their own spiritual misery. This work was carried out through much personal contact and also through the congregation known as the "Oratory."

The exact nature of his vocation had not always been

clear to St. Philip. When he was around 42 years old, after having been a priest for about six years, he and several companions began reading the letters of St. Francis Xavier and other missionaries in India. They became fired with enthusiasm to go to the Far East to save souls and win the crown of martyrdom. But to make sure of God's will, Philip consulted a holy Cistercian who was favored with visions of St. John the Evangelist. The Cistercian reported that St. John had appeared and had delivered this message for Philip: "Rome is to be your Indies."

To the souls in Rome, then, Philip devoted his life. The distinctive mark of his apostolate was cheerfulness, and everyone was captivated by his supernatural charm. Philip soon became the most popular person in the city, and was generally known and loved as "the Apostle of Rome." The improvement in the religious spirit of Rome between the opening and closing years of the 16th century is largely attributable to this one man. By all he did to sanctify Rome, St. Philip Neri exerted an incalculable influence for good upon the Universal Church, which owes him—even to our own time—a debt of unimaginable magnitude.

—The Publishers
April 5, 1984

PREFACE

SINCE the middle of the last century a number of lives of St Philip have appeared in English. The first was a translation of that written by Giacomo Bacci, a father of the Roman Oratory, in 1622, with additions by the Dominican Ricci and others, which has formed the basis of most lives of the Saint written since that date. The translation was by Fr. Faber, begun even before he was a Catholic, and appeared in two volumes, the first of the ' Oratorian ' or ' black ' Lives of the Saints, which were issued between 1847 and 1856, first raising a storm, and afterwards enjoying a considerable success. There have been various subsequent editions of this life, but the last is now out of print. In 1882 there was published in two volumes a translation, by Fr. Thomas Alder Pope, of the Birmingham Oratory, of the admirable Life of St Philip by Alfonso Capecelatro, a father of the Naples Oratory, later a Cardinal and Archbishop of Capua. A new edition of this translation, slightly abbreviated, appeared in 1926 in one volume (London, Burns Oates and Washbourne Ltd., 15s.), while *Pippo Buono*, by Fr. Ralph Kerr, of the London Oratory, described by its author as ' a simple life of St Philip,' and dedicated by him to the children of the Oratory schools, reached a second edition in 1927 (London, Sands & Co., 3s. 6d.). Much earlier than either of these books—probably about 1868—a Mrs. Hope wrote a short Life of St Philip which was quite excellent in its way, but after having passed through various editions it, too, is out of print. In 1927 a work by two French priests,

Louis Ponelle and Louis Bordet, was published with the title, *S. Philip Neri and the Roman Society of his Times* (English translation by Fr. Ralph Kerr, London, Sheed & Ward, 1933, 16s.). In this book the authors, instead of merely repeating what other biographers had said, went back to all the original documents—the process of canonization, contemporary letters, etc.—and produced an enormous amount of interesting matter about St Philip and the times in which he lived. But both this book and the Life by Capecelatro are large volumes—each six hundred pages—and proportionately expensive, while Fr. Kerr's *Pippo Buono* is directed expressly to children.

It remains, therefore, that since the last edition of Mrs. Hope's little book was exhausted, there has been no short life of St Philip on the same lines available for those unable to afford the money to buy or the time required for reading the larger books. A life of this kind is what I am venturing to offer here. Having neither the talent for original research nor the taste for any novel ' interpretation ' of St Philip, I have tried only to give some account of his life and work in the traditional order, following Bacci and Capecelatro, but very briefly and in ordinary language. At the same time I have embodied as much as possible, within the space, of the new information provided by the researches of the Abbés Ponnelle and Bordet, using it where necessary to correct the facts and dates given by earlier writers. To their most valuable work, therefore, as well as to the earlier Lives, I wish to make my very fullest acknowledgements. Lastly, I must express my gratitude to Fr. Denis Sheil, of the Birmingham Oratory, for very kindly helping me with suggestions and criticisms.

ST PHILIP NERI

ST PHILIP NERI

I

THE second child and elder son of Ser Francesco di Filippo of Castelfranco, a citizen of Florence living in the parish of San Pier Gattolini, was born in the year 1515, on July 21, at the sixth hour of the night : according to our reckoning that would be about two o'clock in the morning of July 22, the feast of St Mary Magdalen. That morning he was carried to the ancient baptistery before the doors of the cathedral, and there received in baptism the names Filippo Romolo.

His father was a notary, a profession which would give him a certain standing in Florence, since it was one of the seven greater arts the practice of which qualified a man for the magistracy ; but he was not a successful notary and remained always a poor man. His daughter Caterina was older than Philip, while Lisabetta was younger than he. The fourth child, Antonio, did not long survive his birth, so that with Philip the family came to an end. His mother, Lucrezia da Mosciano, Philip can hardly have known, since she died soon after the birth of Antonio in 1520, but later on his father married again a woman of happy disposition with whom Philip was on excellent terms, and she, on her part, was devoted to him. She asked for him on her death-bed. In the same year that Philip's mother died the family went to live on the slope above the Arno, on the south side of the river, known as the Costa San Giorgio. From this position they would enjoy a glorious view across the river upon the city spread out before them, and beyond it to the hill crowned by the little city of Fiesole.

Philip was by all accounts a handsome boy with attractive manners and a gay spirit, but sensitive— the kind that quickly wins affection from others. It is a testimony both to this quality and to his good behaviour that he acquired among the citizens of Florence the name of ' Pippo Buono.' He never spoke of being a priest or a monk, and was not given to childish pieties such as dressing little altars and the like. But he was fond of visiting the churches of the city, and one likes to picture him praying, or sitting quietly in a corner of Santo Spirito, his mind rested by its cool colouring and harmonious design, or wandering through the spaces of the Duomo, his eye delighted by the frescoes of Giotto in S. Croce, or his heart stirred by those which the Blessed Fra Angelico had painted—often on his knees—in cloister, chapter-room and dormitory at S. Marco.

Here above all it was he loved to come ; and he had special friends among the Dominican fathers of this convent. This friendship with the Order of Preachers lasted all his life, and in later years he used to say to the fathers at the Minerva in Rome : ' All the good I ever had in me from my youth upwards, I owe to your fathers at S. Marco.' From them, too, he learned to venerate a character singularly unlike his own, the severe and stormy reformer, Girolamo Savonarola, who had died seventeen years before Philip was born.

There is one anecdote about his boyhood which no biographer omits. One day when he was about eight years old Philip had been taken by his parents to Castelfranco, in the valley of the Arno, whence the family had originally sprung, and where his father still owned some property, and had been left for a little while in the courtyard of the house to amuse himself. But what could be more amusing to any little boy than to jump on the back of a donkey standing there, loaded with fruit and vegetables? Unfortunately, it happened that the donkey was standing near the top of a flight of stone steps leading to a cellar, and as Philip jumped on its back, down the steps they fell, the donkey, the fruit and Philip, and in such a way that the donkey and the fruit were on top, and Philip underneath. Everyone expected to find Philip dead ; but when he was extracted, not only was he alive, but almost entirely unhurt. He always looked on his preservation on this occasion as a miracle, for which he never forgot to thank God.

Remembering the kind of thing that writers say about the childhood of some saints, one cannot help feeling the kind of satisfaction that one is not, perhaps, meant to feel in finding it related that one day Philip gave his elder sister a push, because she persisted in interrupting when he was trying to recite some Psalms with Lisabetta ! But the Saint's biographers, having felt bound in conscience to record this much, hasten to add that he afterwards bitterly bewailed his fault. He felt no regret for having on another occasion torn up a copy of the family tree given him by his father.

Beyond such incidents as these, recalled by witnesses years later at the process of his canonization, and the fact that he went to school in Florence, we know no details of Philip's life till he was about eighteen years old, when he left Florence to seek his fortune with his uncle Romolo, who was in business at San Germano (now Cassino) in the Kingdom of Naples, at the foot of the hill crowned by St Benedict's glorious abbey. Uncle Romolo, who, as a matter of fact, was not an uncle at all except by courtesy, but some kind of cousin, was reputed to have a considerable fortune, and as he was childless it was hoped that he might eventually make Philip his heir. And so he set out from his native city.

But though he was never to see Florence again, he never forgot that he was a Florentine. It was with a Florentine family that he first made his home in Rome ; the young men in the houses of Florentine bankers were the first objects of his lay apostolate ; he undertook, at the request of his fellow-citizens, the charge of their church of S. Giovanni in Rome. And was it not the Archbishop of Florence who laid the first stone of the new church of S. Maria in Vallicella, and said the first Mass in it when it was completed ?

At San Germano there occurred some sort of spiritual crisis in Philip's life, though we are left in ignorance as to its precise nature, since he was always so reticent about himself and his own experiences that he gave no more than hints even to his most intimate friends. There is a difficulty also about the length of his stay with his uncle. On the one hand, his sister deposed that he left Florence at the age of eighteen—that is in the year 1533—on the other, it is generally agreed that 1533 was the year of his arrival in Rome, and he himself spoke of his business career as having lasted only 'a few days.' Italians, however, are very vague about time : to be asked to wait *un momentino*—a diminutive moment—means, often, that one is expected to wait the best part of an hour. It would not seem unreasonable, therefore, to assume that 'a few days ' might be used vaguely to cover a stay of, perhaps, some months, a period which would suffice for the veracity of the traditional story of how his resolution to leave the world and serve God alone was taken.

It is this. Close to Gaetà, about fifteen miles from Cassino, is a mountain split by three fissures, caused, tradition says, by the quaking of the earth at the hour of our Lord's death, and on this mountain is a sanctuary dedicated to the Holy Trinity, belonging to the Benedictine monks of Monte Cassino. In the main fissure a fallen mass of rock had become firmly wedged, and on this rock a circular chapel had been built, and dedicated to the Holy Cross. To this chapel, reached by an iron ladder, Philip used to come to pray in quiet and solitude. Whether it was the result of some sudden and extraordinary mystical experience, or whether it came only through the gradually deepening understanding and conviction as to God's will, by which the Holy Spirit ordinarily speaks to a soul disposed to receive his inspirations, here, at any rate, the decision was made. He would leave his uncle and any prospects of wealth that his uncle could hold out to him, and set out for Rome, to do whatever God should call him to do. He would never forget his uncle's kindness, he assured him in reply to attempts at dissuasion, but as to the rest, he was more pleased with his affection than with his advice.

II

PHILIP'S LIFE IN ROME AS A LAYMAN

WE must not picture the Rome that Philip entered in 1533 as the city it was to become, even during his life-time, under such great building Popes as Sixtus V. Everywhere ruined palaces and profaned churches still bore witness to what the city had suffered during the Sack of 1527, at the hands of the troops of the Constable of Bourbon. Rome had only just begun to live again its normal life, and it would be long before the traces of the devastation would be covered up.

Nor was the religious atmosphere of Rome comparable with that which was introduced by the reforms effected under such Popes as Paul IV, Pius IV and St Pius V. The spirit prevailing in the highest ecclesiastical circles in 1533 was, unhappily, not vastly different from that which had prevailed in the years immediately preceding the Sack. There were many in the Church who desired reform : St Cajetan and Pietro Carafa, the future Paul IV, had founded the Theatine Order in Rome even before the Sack ; the Barnabites had been founded in Milan, and St Ignatius was gathering disciples in Paris ; but the great movement for reform had not yet got under way in the city of the Popes. Philip himself was to be prominent amongst those principally responsible for the spreading of a new spirit in Rome.

A kindly Florentine named Galeotto del Caccia, an official in the custom-house, living in the piazza of S. Eustachio, gave Philip a little room and a small yearly allowance of corn, in return for which Philip took charge of Caccia's two little boys. This room contained only a bed, a table and a chair, with a cord from wall to wall on which to hang his clothes, and a shelf for a few books ; but it was Philip's home from the time of his arrival in Rome till his ordination, a period of nearly eighteen years. His allowance of corn he took to a neighbouring baker, who gave him every day a small roll of bread. This, with a few olives, was his sole food, and he ate standing by a well from which he drew water to drink ; sometimes he went as long as three days altogether without food. No wonder he could say in later life that in his youth he had lived on only a few sixpences a month. His two pupils both eventually became ecclesiastics : Michele a secular priest and rector of S. Donato at Citille, near Florence, and Ippolito, a Carthusian.

Beginning, probably, in 1534, Philip followed the course of philosophy at the university of the Sapienza, and subsequently the course of theology under the Augustinian fathers at S. Agostino.

The knowledge of theology which he later showed himself to possess was not inconsiderable, for we are told that he had a special predilection for the *Summa* of St Thomas, and that he had it constantly in his hands. The facility and correctness with which, as a priest, he could discuss the most difficult questions, sometimes surprised those who judged him by his outward simplicity.

His studies, however, were not allowed to interfere with his prayer ; rather was the contrary the case.

For, as he admitted, a certain crucifix in the Augustinian schools so held his attention that he could do nothing but sigh and weep. In the end it was this attraction that conquered. After a few years— probably in 1537—he sold his books and broke off his studies, as he had previously broken off his business career, to give himself up wholly to the things of the spirit.

For the next ten years his life was to be that of a hermit in everything except that he retained his room in the Caccia household. Everywhere and at all times prayer came easily to him—in his little room, in the streets, in the churches (or in their porches if they were closed)—but, above all, it was in solitary places and at night that he loved to pray. And so there began those extraordinary nocturnal expeditions out into the Roman Campagna, sometimes to make the pilgrimage to the Seven Churches, sometimes to visit some other place with holy associations. Most often of all it was to the basilica of S. Sebastiano, out on the Appian Way, that he turned his steps, to spend whole nights in the catacombs beneath the church ; so frequently, in fact, that he was later pointed out by the Dominican novice-master as having ' lived ' for ten whole years in the caves of S. Sebastiano. Nor were these nocturnal pilgrimages entirely without their alarms, for did he not one night see devils near the Capo di Bove, as it is called—the tomb of Cecilia Metella beside the Appian Way, only a short distance beyond S. Sebastiano ?

One particular chapel in these same catacombs of S. Sebastiano (now marked by a bust of St Philip) was to be the scene of an extraordinary experience, which was at once the reward of his fervour in prayer and the cause of its still further increase. The details of this experience Philip himself confided to Cardinal Federigo Borromeo in his old age.

He was twenty-nine years old at the time, and as the feast of Pentecost was approaching, Philip, who had always had a special devotion to the Holy Spirit, was praying with extreme earnestness for his gifts and graces, when he seemed to see a globe of fire which entered his mouth and sank down into his heart. At the same time he was pervaded by a fire of love which seemed to be a positive physical heat, so that he had to throw himself on the ground and bare his breast to cool it. When he rose he was seized with a violent trembling, accompanied by an extraordinary sense of joy, and putting his hand to his heart, he felt there a swelling as big as a man's fist.

After his death it was discovered that the first two of the false ribs were broken, and the broken ends thrust outwards, never having rejoined or returned to the normal position during the fifty remaining years of Philip's life. At the same time there began that palpitation of the heart which lasted throughout his life, and made itself felt particularly when he was praying, hearing confessions, saying Mass or giving Communion, or when he was speaking on some subject which stirred his emotions. So violent was this palpitation that it was described by those who knew him best as being like the blows of a hammer, while the trembling it caused was such as to shake his chair, his bed, or sometimes even the whole room. Yet, when he pressed his penitents to his heart, they felt an extraordinary consolation, and many learned by experience that to be pressed to Philip's heart was the most effective way of being delivered from temptation.

Besides these palpitations Philip always felt a sense of burning heat in the region of the heart and throat. His almost incredibly spare diet was due to the fact that he thought this to be the best means of reducing this heat ; and for the same purpose he had himself bled frequently, and was given cooling medicines. Even in the depths of winter he had his windows wide open at night, and when there was snow on the ground he strolled through the streets of Rome with his cassock unbuttoned, laughing at his young men because they were less able to bear the cold than he. In the pontificate of Gregory XIII an order was issued that all confessors were to wear the cotta in the confessional, whereupon Philip presented himself before the Pope with his cassock unbuttoned in the same way, and succeeded in obtaining a special exemption for himself.

This remarkable gift was followed by such an access of fervour that it became almost more than he could bear. On one occasion in particular, he was forced to throw himself on the ground and cry out : ' I cannot bear so much, my God, I cannot bear so much, for see, I am dying of it.' Thenceforward, we are told, God mitigated the intensity of his sensible devotion, so that in his latter years he used to say, ' I had more fervour when I was young than I have now.'

But love, as St Teresa says, ' is always working in a thousand different ways.' Even before this extraordinary gift of the Holy Spirit, from the very beginning of his hermit life, Philip had been drawn to that work of charity which he was later to commend so insistently to his disciples, for the good of their own souls as well as for the good of those they served—the work of the hospitals. To the great hospital known as S. Giacomo degli Incurabili in particular, it seems, all those were sooner or later drawn who, in the midst of the corruptions of the time, were trying to rekindle the flame of Christian charity in Rome.

To appreciate what this means it must be remembered that hospital visiting at that time had a very different connotation from that which it has for us. It was not a matter of bringing the patients a few grapes, with a bright smile, but of sweeping the floors of the wards, feeding and washing the patients, and rendering them every kind of service, besides seeing that they received the sacraments if they were in danger of death. Philip lived to see the administration of the hospitals vastly improved under the reforming Popes yet to come ; and it was a penitent of his, St Camillus of Lellis, who was to found a religious order specifically vowed to the care of the souls and bodies of the sick—the *Camillini*, as the Italians call them, or Clerks Regular Servants of the Sick. But at this period the work of the hospitals was one which needed all that generous charity with which Philip's heart was now still more completely filled.

Sometimes, also, on his visits to the churches of the city, Philip used to stop to instruct some of the beggars and idlers who loitered about the porticos ; but the special form his lay apostolate took was an indirect one. That personal charm which all who came into contact with him, at whatever period of his life, found so irresistible—and young men particularly—was first exercised upon the young

Florentines, men of his own nation, employed in the warehouses, banks and shops of Rome. Having established a personal influence over them, Philip used it to persuade them to live lives more consistent with the faith which they all had deep down in their hearts : ' Well, my brothers,' he used to say, ' and when shall we begin to do good ? '

In this way he won, among others whose names we know, both Teseo Raspa and Enrico Pietra, who were later to be colleagues of his as priests at S. Girolamo della Carità. Pietra eventually founded the Congregation of Christian Doctrine, with Philip's active assistance. But a more remarkable conversion was that of Prospero Crivelli, the chief cashier of one of the leading banks in Rome. Things had gone so far with him that he had been refused absolution by his Jesuit confessor. He confided in Philip, who did what he could to console him, and promised to pray for him : ' I will pray so hard,' he said, ' that you will give up your occasion of sin at once.' And he was as good as his word. Prospero was soon disposed to do what was necessary, and received absolution ; and thereafter, following Philip's advice in everything, he became a model of virtue and a genuinely spiritual man.

It is to this period of Philip's life that his contact with St Ignatius is to be assigned. A number of those whom he was instrumental in converting became members of religious orders, and some among them joined the Company of Jesus. Philip himself said that he had been the first to send Italians to join the Company ; yet the invitation to join it himself he could not accept : he was, the founder of the Company said, like the church bell, which calls others to enter but itself stays outside.

Philip admired Ignatius, and spoke in later years of having seen his face ' all resplendent,' as he saw the faces of the Carthusians at S. Maria degli Angeli as they came from prayer. But if Philip ' stayed outside ' the Company, who can wonder at it ? We say in the office of confessor bishops, ' *Non est inventus similis illi* '—there is none found like to him—it is, therefore, in no sense derogatory to either Saint to say that in temperament, in habit of mind, in method and in the spirit which each left as a legacy to his sons, Philip and Ignatius were as dissimilar as any two men very well could be who were both priests, both working to some extent in the same sphere, and both one day to be canonized.

From the year 1548 onwards Philip's zeal was directed into a more clearly defined channel. On August 16 in that year, in conjunction with his confessor, Persiano Rosa, he laid the foundations of a work which was to become famous as the Trinità de' Pellegrini.

This Persiano Rosa, an admirable priest of cheerful temperament, had grouped round himself about a dozen laymen, who met for prayer in common and spiritual conversations, received Holy Communion on Sundays and feast days—a frequency that was quite exceptional in those days—and assisted at the Offices in the church of S. Girolamo della Carità, to which Rosa was attached. It was now resolved that they should be canonically erected as a confraternity, and that they should undertake the charitable work of assisting the poor pilgrims who arrived in Rome from distant countries worn out, penniless, and often ill.

A start was made with a hired house, to which

another had soon to be added, in the Jubilee year of
1550. Other helpers came forward, so that the
work extended rapidly, and it was soon decided
that, during the periods between the years when
there was a great influx of pilgrims, their house
should be used to lodge convalescents—those, that
is, who were discharged often far too soon from the
hospitals, so that if they had nowhere to go there
was every probability of their relapsing. The full
title of the confraternity thus became : ' della SS.
Trinità de' Pellegrini e de' Convalescenti.' The
badge of the confraternity shows the Eternal Father
above the Eternal Son on the Cross, with the Holy
Spirit in the form of a dove between them, while at
the foot of the Cross St Philip kneels in priest's
vestments. In the same Jubilee year the seat of the
confraternity was transferred to the little church of
S. Salvatore in Campo, which thus became the
scene of an interesting and important development in the devotional life of the city.

For, in spite of its increasing external works and
growing numbers, the confraternity never lost
sight of its original spiritual ideal, and it was the
members of the Trinità de' Pellegrini who first
introduced into Rome the devotion of the Quarant'
Ore—the forty continuous hours of prayer before
the Blessed Sacrament—which had originated in
Milan. From the year 1551, most probably, they
practised this devotion on the first Sunday of every
month. Philip preached little sermons to stir up
the fervour of the brothers, though sometimes they
had a still wider effect ; for on one occasion, we are
told, his words converted ' thirty dissolute youths.'
He himself hardly left the church at all while the
devotion lasted, but called the relays of watchers

with a little bell. To those whose turn was finished he used to say : ' Away, my brothers, the hour of prayer is finished, but the time for doing good is not finished yet.'

In the foundation of the confraternity he had been advised and helped by Persiano Rosa. But the counsel of this discerning priest was to lead Philip further still. He had been happy in his life and work as a layman, and apparently would have wished to continue in that state ; but Persiano Rosa was himself persuaded, and succeeded in persuading Philip, that if he was to use to the full the talents God had given him, if his power for good was to have its full scope, he ought to be a priest. Rosa gave him such instruction as was then considered necessary and sufficient (it will be remembered that he had already followed courses of philosophy and theology) and in 1551 Philip was ordained—to the minor orders and subdiaconate in March, at the little church of S. Tommaso in Parione, to the diaconate on Holy Saturday, March 29, at the Lateran, and again at S. Tommaso in Parione, on May 23, to the priesthood.

III

AFTER his ordination Philip went to live at
S. Girolamo della Carità. This little church,
which stood on the traditional site of the house of
St Paula, where she was visited by St Jerome, was
the headquarters of an important Archconfraternity
of Charity. Persiano Rosa, Philip's confessor, was
one of the chaplains of this confraternity, and
Francesco Marsuppini, who was to become his
confessor after Rosa's death, was another, and it was
probably through their influence that Philip was
aggregated to their community. Not that it was a
religious community in the ordinary sense of the
word, since there was neither common table nor
superior, properly speaking ; and while some of
them received a salary besides their lodging,
others received only their lodging.

Philip was of the latter class, which meant that
he was free from any definite obligations, but that
he had to support himself. Nor was this difficult,
since he required so little. His server brought him
every day two little loaves and a flask of wine ;
this formed the main meal of the day, which he took
standing, with a little napkin spread, in the sacristy
after his Mass. If he received any other present of
food, he gave it away to the boys who served the
other Masses, and in a year of scarcity, when some-

one sent him six loaves, he gave them all away to a Spanish priest in the community, because he thought that this foreigner would find greater difficulty in obtaining food than he would himself.

S. Girolamo della Carità, then a little basilica with three naves in the regular Roman style (it was rebuilt in 1609), lay only a short way off the then fashionable via Giulia and the Campo de' Fiori. It was much frequented, both because the church was devotional, and because the chaplains serving it were priests of good reputation. The outstanding personality amongst them was Buonsignore Cacciaguerra, a convert from a life of luxury and libertinage, who was now ardently propagating the practice of frequent, and even daily Communion —a thing then almost unheard of—in which he was to receive active support from Philip. Philip himself said Mass every day, and wished that other priests should do so. The excuses of those who refrained from saying Mass on the pretext of rest or recreation did not commend themselves to him : ' The soul that seeks recreation out of the Creator, and consolation out of Christ, will never find them,' he used to say.

His own extraordinary fervour in celebrating, do what he might to control it, was known to everyone, and was an embarrassment to himself. He is unique, I think, among the Saints in having it recorded of him that, so far from having to recollect himself in preparation for Mass, he had sometimes to have frivolous books read to him in order to bring him down to earth enough to enable him to attend properly to the external actions of the Sacrifice. But even so, the server would often have to pull his vestments to remind him what to do next, and his trembling and palpitation would come on so violently at the offertory that he had to rest his arm on the altar to steady it in pouring in the wine and water. At the elevation he lowered the Host quickly, lest he should find himself unable to lower it at all, and at the Communion he so clung to his chalice that he wore off the gilding, and left the marks of his teeth on it. At times, too, he was seen to be raised up from the predella, so that he appeared to be dancing on his toes ; this made a little girl one day think—and say—that he must be possessed.

In order to prevent himself from being carried away, besides his singular preparation for Mass, he used to go through all the actions as rapidly as possible. Sometimes he would stamp his feet, or tell those near by to ' drive away those dogs,' and once, while reading the Passion in Holy Week, he played all the time with the key of his room. To prevent others from watching the extraordinary effects of his devotion, he generally said the last Mass, when there were fewest people in church ; he pre-ferred to celebrate at the high altar, and would not let the server kneel where he could see his face. Finally, in his old age he was given the privilege of saying Mass in a private chapel.

From the first year of his priesthood dates also Philip's unwearying assiduity in the work of the confessional, a work in which his zeal never slack-ened, so that he could scarcely be induced to give it up even when he was really ill. If his doctors suggested that it tired him too much, he declared that it was rather a relief and recreation : ' It is the greatest pleasure to me,' he used to say, ' even to sit in the confessional.'

In those early days at S. Girolamo he would go down to the church first thing in the morning to his confessional, and scarcely stir from it till noon, his usual time for saying Mass. If no one came he would stay near his confessional reading, or saying his office or rosary ; or he would walk a little way outside the church, so that casual passers-by could see that he was available.

Soon, however, there was never any lack of penitents. Those who went to Philip once, especially if they were young men, were conscious of some peculiar attraction in him which brought them back to him again and again, so that before long it was no extraordinary thing for him to have heard as many as forty confessions in his room before going down to the church. For the benefit of these early-comers he used to leave the key under the door of his room. And as these young men attached themselves to him, so would he expend the most affectionate care on them. It was not enough just to hear their confessions, advise and absolve them ; he wished to have them under his eye during what he considered the most dangerous time of the day, if it was un-occupied—the hours after the midday meal. He therefore used to invite a number of them to his room, where they would read some book such as the *Conferences* of Cassian, or the *Lives of the Saints*, and then converse on some point arising out of what they had read. Philip would generally lean against his bed, and would sometimes be seized with his palpitations and fits of trembling so violently as to shake the whole room. After the conversations they used to go for a walk together, perhaps to visit some church or other, and some of them would go back again with Philip to S. Girolamo for prayer in the evening. These two features, the conversations in the afternoon and the prayer in the evening, are of great importance ; they are the germ of all that the Oratory was to become in its most essential elements.

The original group cannot have numbered more than eight in all, and they were nearly all young Tuscans of the kind that Philip gathered in the shops and banks—there were two goldsmiths and one hosier amongst those whose names have been preserved. But it was not long before other penitents of Philip's and their friends were drawn into the circle, so that first an adjoining room had to be pressed into service to contain them, and when this too overflowed, Philip built a room—or more probably adapted some already existing space in the roof of the church—for this purpose. In this Oratory, as they called it, the meetings became more definitely organized. Instead of the informal conversations, different speakers discoursed in turn in the afternoon, while the evening meetings for prayer also became a regular feature and acquired a fixed form. But before we follow out these new developments, it is necessary to say something about the opposition that Philip had to contend with before his work was firmly established, as well as something about certain of these new-comers.

For it was not everyone who regarded with favour Philip's encouragement of all and sundry to frequent the sacraments, and his readiness to administer them at all times. Possibly some of the chaplains feared that the practice followed by Philip and Cacciaguerra of saying Mass every day might lead to the establishment of a custom which would add to their own obligations. At any rate, it was not long before a positive persecution was launched against both of them.

The instigator of the persecution appears to have been a physician, Vincenzo Teccosi, who was one of the ' deputies ' (a kind of board of managers) administering the affairs of the Archconfraternity of Charity ; but his principal agents were two clerics employed in the sacristy. These two clerics were, as a matter of fact, priests and ' apostates,' as they were called in the language of the times—religious, that is, who had deserted from their monasteries—and their position as sacristans gave them the opportunity to insult and harass Philip in the kind of way he would feel most acutely. Sometimes they would refuse to give him vestments, or gave him only those that were old and shabby ; or they would send him to one altar and then, when he was about to begin, send him to another, or back to the sacristy. At the same time calumnies were put about, in order to shake the confidence of their followers in the two priests.

The intention was, of course, to force them to leave S. Girolamo altogether, and some of Philip's friends seem to have urged him to do so ; but his own course was to accept every humiliation with meekness and resignation. One day at Mass, we are told, when he felt he had almost reached the limits of his endurance, he fixed his eyes on the crucifix and said : ' Good Jesus, why do you not hear me ? So long and so earnestly have I asked patience of you. Why have you not heard me ? ' At once he seemed to hear a voice which said : ' You ask patience of me ? Be sure that I will give it you ; but this is the means by which it is my will that you should gain it.' In the event Philip's patience lasted longer than his opponents' ill-will. First one and then the other of the sacristans repented (they finally returned to their religious houses) and at length Teccosi publicly asked Philip's forgiveness, and afterwards became one of his most devoted disciples. Nor was this all, for, on the intervention of the Cardinal Protector of the Archconfraternity, it was decided that for the future the chaplains at S. Girolamo should have a definite superior, and the first superior to be selected was no other than Philip's fellow-victim in the persecution, Buonsignore Cacciaguerra.

IV

PHILIP thus found himself free to develop his work in his own way, with a steadily growing circle of followers, who now included, in addition to the original group, a number of men of distinction from the circles of the papal court.

Giambattista Salviati, for instance, was the brother of Cardinal Giovanni Salviati, a nephew of Leo X and a cousin of Catherine de' Medici, Queen of France, but a worldly and dissolute character when he was first brought to Philip. After his conversion not only was he much given to prayer and mortification, but he was sent, like the rest of Philip's penitents, to serve the sick in the hospitals. An old servant of his, whom he found in the hospital della Consolazione, could with difficulty be induced to believe that this relation of queens and cardinals was not making game of him when he came to make his bed. Yet—and this is typical of Philip's methods—when Salviati wished to dispense with the retinue of servants that it was then considered necessary for a nobleman to have following him through the streets, Philip would not consent. The change he wished to bring about was an interior change, and he was always opposed to any hurried change in the external conditions of a man's life where these were not in themselves sinful.

It was Costanzo Tassone who had brought

Salviati to Philip. He and yet another of Philip's converts, Felice Figliucci, were members of the household of Cardinal Sforza di Santa Fiora. The Cardinal was not overpleased at his servants being turned into devotees, or taken away from him ; for Tassone later became a priest and entered the service of St Charles Borromeo. And Santa Fiora had another cause for complaint. One day Tassone took the Cardinal's little dog, Capriccio, on a visit to Philip, and from that day forward nothing could induce the dog to leave him. Capriccio died eventually in Philip's room, after doing good service for many years as an instrument of mortification to the many smart young men who used to be sent to take him for a walk, or made to groom him.

Incidentally it is interesting to find noted as a trait in Philip's character (whose whole temperament was certainly *italianissimo*) a fondness for animals such as we are apt to consider a peculiarly English characteristic. For besides Capriccio there was a cat of whom he took the greatest care. When he left S. Girolamo she stayed behind, but every day one of his young men had to take her to dinner, and Philip required a detailed account of her health and appetite. He also accepted the present of two little birds from a young Frenchman, on the condition that he came every day to attend to them—a device, no doubt, for securing his own hold over the young man—and one day when he came he found them perched on Philip himself and singing. On the other hand, a father of his Congregation, in later years, was sharply rebuked for thoughtless cruelty in crushing a lizard with his foot ; and he spoke no less freely to a butcher whom he saw ill-treating a dog.

More important than either Salviati or Tassone was the conquest of Francesco Maria Tarugi. He came from Montepulciano, and was related to two Popes—Julius III and Marcellus II. Handsome and well built, with charming manners and an exceptional gift of natural eloquence, his success as a courtier would have been assured. But on the occasion of a Jubilee published by Paul IV he made a general confession to Philip, who took the words out of his mouth, and revealed to him his most secret thoughts. In the hour of prayer that he spent with him afterwards Tarugi experienced such spiritual delight that, though he had not the courage at once to shake himself free from certain entanglements, everything that had up till now delighted him became a source of torment. Within a few months circumstances delivered him from the entanglement, as Philip had foretold would happen —in fact, death removed the lady who constituted it—and his conversion was completed. He became the most distinguished preacher that the Oratory had, and always seems to have retained the position of Philip's favourite son. Many years later, when he was a Cardinal and Archbishop of Avignon, it was his boast that for fifty years he had been Philip's novice.

Of a different type was Giovan Battista Modio, a physician and an author, who later on produced a commentary on the canticles of the Blessed Jacopone da Todi, one of the favourite books for spiritual reading at the Oratory. He was once suddenly cured when in great pain from stone and apparently dying, and always attributed his recovery to Philip, who, after paying him a visit, had gone to a neighbouring church and was praying for him with great vehemence. It fell to him to relate the lives of the Saints in the Oratory, and after his death another doctor, Antonio Fucci, succeeded him in this office.

But besides these distinguished men there were other very simple souls, who loved Philip and in whom he delighted. There was Stefano the shoemaker, for instance, full of enmities and hatreds till he went to S. Girolamo and was won by Philip, and ' il Ferrarese,' who heard the angels sing and had the gift of tears when he communicated. Tommaso, too, a Sicilian, the summit of whose ambition was attained when he became a sweeper of St Peter's. He slept in his clothes on the predella of one of the seven altars, and never left the basilica except to go to confession to Philip. Fra Ludovico— not really a friar but a poor man who wore the Franciscan habit—was so virtuous that Philip put him in charge of the girls at S. Caterina de' Funari, an institute founded by St Ignatius, while Pietro Molinaro lost his sight through the abundance of the tears he shed, but had it restored by a miracle.

It is noteworthy that, though later on we find Philip on warmly affectionate terms with a number of good women of all sorts who were his penitents, there are comparatively few that we hear of at this period besides Porzia de' Massimi, the wife of Giambattista Salviati, who had already been led to a spiritual life by Philip and helped him to gain her husband, and Fiora Ragni, the ' Madonna Fiora ' to whom one of his few extant letters is addressed. But one incident of a type not unusual in Saints' lives probably belongs to the early period of Philip's priesthood.

An abandoned woman, who lived in the via

Giulia, boasted that the virtue of this priest who was so much talked of would not be proof against her charms. She therefore gave it out that she was ill and wished to change her life, if Philip would come and hear her confession. When he arrived, however, she advanced to meet him wearing only a transparent veil, and he turned and fled. So furious was the woman that she caught up the first thing to hand—it happened to be a heavy stool—and flung it after Philip. He came away unharmed ; but it was a maxim that he was fond of impressing on others afterwards that, in the battle with the temptations of the flesh, it is cowards—those who run away, that is—who are the victors.

A more subtle temptation—for it was in effect a temptation against the vocation which God had marked out for him—arose from the spiritual reading at the conferences in his room. For besides such books as the life of Blessed Giovanni Colombini and the canticles of the Blessed Jacopone da Todi, they had read aloud the letters of St Francis Xavier and the Jesuit missionaries from India. Fired with enthusiasm at the thought of the enormous harvest to be reaped in the Far East, Philip began to think that he, too, ought to go to the Indies, to share in the labour and in the chance of winning the crown of martyrdom. As many as twenty of his circle declared themselves ready and anxious to go with him. Yet he would not take so serious a step, involving others besides himself, without making quite sure that it was an inspiration from God that he should take it. He therefore prayed about it very earnestly, and also went to consult a Benedictine monk at the abbey of St Paul's outside the walls. The Benedictine sent him on to the Tre

Fontane to consult Vincenzo Ghettini, the prior of the Cistercians there, a man of great sanctity who was favoured with visions of St John the Evangelist. The answer was not given at once ; Philip was to come back again after a few days. When he returned the Cistercian told him that St John had appeared to him and had given him the answer. It was : ' Rome is to be your Indies.'

Truly, there was enough that needed doing in Rome, and by saving souls there he would please God as well as by saving them elsewhere. The project of going to the Indies was laid aside, and Philip devoted himself to the work that was growing so rapidly around him.

V

ADDITIONS TO PHILIP'S CIRCLE : BARONIUS, PALESTRINA AND OTHERS

IT must have been after this episode (since there is no mention of him amongst those who were ready to go to the Indies) that there was added to Philip's immediate circle a young man who was to become one of the most illustrious members of his Congregation, and, in 1596, a Cardinal. This was Cesare Baronio, more generally known as Baronius, the author of the famous *Annals* and the ' father ' of scientific church history.

He came from the Abruzzi, and had studied law at the University of Naples, but in 1557 left it for Rome, hoping to make a career for himself under the patronage of some Cardinal. He was already in disgrace with his parents over some youthful folly when he arrived in Rome, but still greater was his father's disgust when he learned that, through frequenting the Oratory, his son had come to the resolution of abandoning his career in the world, and was thinking of becoming a religious. As an effective mark of his displeasure he cut off all supplies ; but Philip came to the rescue by obtaining for him the post of tutor to Ottavio Paravicini, another future Cardinal.

Philip used to laugh at this young man, who took everything so very seriously ; and it must have been a very deep humility which could support some of the mortifications with which he tried him. It was he, for instance, who was sent with an enormous bottle to buy half a pint of wine ; he was to insist on the bottle being carefully washed and finally to tender a gold piece in payment. Even worse was the occasion when, in keeping with his serious temperament, he was made to intone the Miserere at a wedding breakfast. But the humble opinion he had of himself, and retained even when he was a famous man and the friend of other famous men, his simplicity and complete disinterestedness, were just such qualities as Philip most desired in his sons ; and it was Baronius who, after periods in which his submissive loyalty must have been strained to the utmost, was designated by Philip as the best fitted to be his own successor, when he laid down the government of his Congregation three years before he died.

It is to Baronius that we owe the description of the afternoon exercises in the Oratory above the church of S. Girolamo when, with the increase in numbers, they had assumed a definite form : ' After some time spent in mental prayer one of the brothers read a spiritual book, and in the middle of the reading the Father who superintended the whole discoursed upon what was read, explaining it with greater accuracy, enlarging upon it and inculcating it into the hearts of the hearers. Sometimes he desired one of the brothers to give his opinion on the subject, and then the discourse proceeded in the form of a dialogue ; and this exercise lasted an hour, to the great consolation of the audience. After this one of his own people, at his command, mounted to a seat raised a few steps above the rest, and without any adornment of language discoursed upon some approved lives of the Saints, illustrating what was said by passages of Scripture, or sentences from the fathers. He was succeeded by another, in the same style, but on a different subject ; and lastly came a third, who discoursed upon ecclesiastical history. When all this was finished, to the wonderful contentment as well as profit of the hearers, they sang some spiritual canticle, prayed again for a short time, and so the exercise ended.'

The ' third, who discoursed upon ecclesiastical history ' was, of course, Baronius himself. His natural inclination was to deliver terrifying discourses on death, judgment and hell, but Philip had other ideas for him, and insisted that Baronius, in spite of his repugnance, should study the history of the Church, and relate it day by day in the Oratory. It was not until he had related the whole course of the church's history seven times over, during a space extending over twenty-seven years, that he began to prepare for publication the fruits of the researches in which his study had involved him, researches which he pursued with the most conscientious care, taking it for his rule never to make any statement unless he himself felt sure of its truth. Thus, it was not till 1588 that the first volume of the *Annales Ecclesiasticæ* came from the press, though the rest followed in rapid succession.

They were received at once with universal praise, and the Catholic world was delighted that in the *Annales* it was provided with a documented refutation of the Magdeburg *Centuries*, a Lutheran production in which a travesty of history was made to serve as a weapon against the Catholic Church. Baronius, however, tried to turn aside the praise from himself, declaring in the preface to the eighth volume, which he dedicated as ' A thanksgiving to the Blessed Philip Neri, founder of the Congregation of the Oratory,' what he had been precluded from saying while Philip was alive, that it was Philip rather than he who ought to be regarded as the author of the work. In the course of this long preface he says :

' Being, therefore, under so many obligations to him, I wish, as far as these *Annals* are concerned, that this my thanksgiving should always live and always speak, and I offer it to him, the author of every one of my undertakings, as a sign of eternal remembrance. . . . For it was the Blessed Philip who by Divine inspiration commanded me to perform this work like another Moses, committing to workmen the building of the Tabernacle, according to the model which he had seen on the Mount. I set myself, then, to this great undertaking, after repeated orders from him, very much against my own will, objecting and entirely distrusting my ability for such a work. I undertook it out of obedience to the will of God, and on this ground also he constantly urged me forward whenever, overpowered by my burden, I interrupted the work for a short time, and with sharp rebukes compelled me to resume my task immediately.'

Further on he apostrophizes Philip :

' Thou wert continually by me, spurring me on with thy presence, and urging me forward with thy words, always a stern exactor (forgive me for saying so) of the daily task thou didst require of me. . . . Not only was no companion given me to help me, but, as happened to the children of Israel in Egypt, the labour was increased and no straw given. Many other things were required of me ; to the weighty task of the *Annals* were added the burdens of the care of the souls, preaching, the government of the house and of many other occupations which were daily imposed upon me, now by one and now by another. And so it seemed as if, in thus treating me or letting others do so, thou wert desiring almost anything of me rather than the one thing which beyond all else thou wert demanding.'

Nor did poor Baronius receive any word of praise from Philip when his task was completed. He feared for the humility of his much lauded disciple, and not only was Baronius dispensed from no duty during the writing of the *Annals*, but when each volume was finished, all that he received from Philip was an obedience to serve thirty Masses.

The mention in Baronius' description of the afternoon exercises in the Oratory of the ' spiritual canticle ' which brought the meeting to an end, brings us to the name of the celebrated Giovanni Animuccia. Both he and his wife had been led to the practice of a spiritual life by Philip, and he became a regular frequenter of the Oratory in its earliest days. He held the position of ' maestro di cappella ' to the basilica of St Peter, and always brought with him to the Oratory some of his colleagues, who sang polyphonic motets at the conclusion of the meetings. But besides directing the music there he published three collections of musical compositions specially intended for use at the Oratory, two books of ' Laudi '—a word which covers all kinds of extra-liturgical composi-tions, both what we should call ' popular hymns ' in the vernacular and Latin motets—and a book of ' spiritual madrigals.' He also published books of Masses and Magnificats.

Some of these musicians were often of the party which used to go with Philip, particularly on the eves of the great feasts as a preparation for Holy Communion, to assist at Matins and Lauds in choir with the Dominicans at the Minerva, or with the Capuchins. When this was so they used to join in the singing of Lauds, to the great delight of everyone present.

Though it is rather anticipating events, it may be added here that after the death of Animuccia, which took place in 1571 with Philip at his side, a still more famous musician was intimately connected with the music of the Oratory, and wrote special compositions for it—the great Giovanni Pierluigi da Palestrina. Since Persiano Rosa, Philip's confessor, and Angelo Velli, who later became a father of Philip's Congregation, also came from Palestrina and were intimate friends of Pierluigi, it seems probable that Philip must also have known him well from early days, and the composer's biographers say that he was also a penitent of Philip's, and that he was assisted by him on his death-bed.

But from 1575 onwards Philip's Congregation, which had then just been founded, had its own musician. For in that year there entered it, though without relinquishing his position as a singer in the papal choir, Fr. Francisco Soto, a Spaniard from Langa, who had begun to frequent the Oratory when he first came to Rome in 1562, and formed one of the body of singers under Animuccia. Fr. Soto who, we are told, had a voice which was the admiration of all Rome, published two further collections of ' Laudi ' sung at the Oratory, containing compositions of Animuccia, Palestrina and others too. He was an estimable priest and full of good works, but of great simplicity ; a letter of 1586 says : ' Fr. Soto has also returned from Perugia, with the degree of Doctor in Simplicity.' This is the kind of degree that Philip would have appreciated. It is interesting to note, also, that Fr. Soto was active in founding and furnishing with vocations the first Carmelite convent in Rome of St Teresa's reform, at S. Giuseppe Capo le Case.

VI

THE EXERCISES OF THE ORATORY AND THE PILGRIMAGE
TO THE SEVEN CHURCHES

THE afternoon Oratory, then, in its developed
form consisted of spiritual reading, which led
to informal discourses and discussions, then three
more discourses, each lasting about half an hour,
delivered by speakers who sat on a platform not
much raised above their audience, and finally some
singing, which brought the meeting to an end. At
the same time the evening Oratory also developed
a set procedure. Half an hour's mental prayer was
followed by the recitation of the Litanies, or
similar vocal prayers ; but three times a week,
instead of the Litanies, the door was shut and
the window-shutters closed, so that no light was
visible except one that shone from a little lamp on
to a crucifix, and after the recital of a short narrative
of the Passion all took the discipline for the space of
a Miserere and De Profundis. The evening Oratory
ended with the singing of the antiphon of Our
Lady.

On the mornings of Sundays and feasts particularly, though some came every day, the members
of the Oratory used to meet for Mass and Communion, after which they would divide into three
parties to visit the three great hospitals of the
Lateran, the Madonna della Consolazione and
Santo Spirito. Philip always attached great impor-

tance to this work which he himself had practised as a layman, and he still generally accompanied one of the parties. It was not enough for him that these luxurious young Romans should be converted to the extent of receiving the sacraments and listening to sermons and hymns. He wished that a changed heart should show itself by a wholly different attitude towards life, by a willingness to serve others instead of merely amusing themselves, and a readiness to do the very things they would formerly have considered it degrading to do— above all to be seen doing. And such things they did at Philip's word. One day in the year 1554, as one of these parties was on its way to a hospital and Philip with it, they saw a sick man lying by the roadside. A sign from Philip was enough to make one of these young men hoist the sick man on his shoulders and carry him through the streets to the hospital. The story of Salviati and his old servant has already been told.

These different forms of the exercises all passed eventually into the constitutions of the Congregation of the Oratory, and have all survived in one form or another. The full form of the afternoon exercises, with four sermons in succession, can scarcely have existed anywhere except in Rome in the earliest days, but informal sermons delivered sitting have always been an essential feature of St Philip's Congregations. Similarly, though in different places it has assumed different forms, the mental prayer in common after the evening Ave has always been maintained. In some places a meditation is given publicly in the church, in others the exercises take place in the Oratory properly so called (distinct from the church) to which men only are admitted, and then the primitive form just described is strictly adhered to. On Sunday mornings the Brothers of the Little Oratory, as they are called, meet for Mass and Communion, and there are still, happily, some places where they continue to visit the hospitals and minister to the patients according to St Philip's original plan.

There was one other exercise which became a special devotion of the Oratory, though it was in no sense an invention of Philip's, but an ancient devotion which he repopularized.

The afternoon exercises of the Oratory, it will be remembered, were in their origin a device of Philip's for keeping his young men not only out of mischief, but occupied in a way that was good for them, during what he considered the most dangerous time of the day. But if the day had its especially dangerous times, so had the year, the season of the Carnival in particular, when it was the accepted convention that every kind of moral restraint could be laid aside, and every kind of licence indulged in— as a preparation for keeping a good Lent. No doubt preachers fulminated against the evil, and holy religious made acts of reparation. But who does not know that fulmination against a firmly established popular custom is, as a rule, so much breath wasted? People listen, and perhaps applaud the admirable sentiments expressed and the zeal which gives them expression—and then go on just as before.

But it was never Philip's way to waste time in fulminating against anything in the way of worldly vanity. His methods are exemplified in the story of the young man who wore an inordinately large ruff (of the Walter Raleigh kind) to whom Philip only said, ' If your ruff did not hurt my hands I should be able to caress you more often ' ; or in that of the woman who asked if it was wrong to wear high-heeled shoes, and was told, ' Only take care you don't fall.' ' Only let a little Divine love find an entrance into their hearts,' he used to say, ' and then you may leave them to themselves.' Should he tell these young men that the revelries of the Carnival were almost inevitably a proximate occasion of sin ? They knew that already. Could he tell them to stay at home ? They could scarcely be expected to do so when everyone else was out holiday-making. The more excellent way was to provide a counter-attraction, a day's outing which would strengthen them in their good resolutions instead of leading them to break them. He had made the pilgrimage to the Seven Churches alone so often ; now he would take his penitents and followers with him.

At first the party that went with Philip was only a small one, but in successive years the numbers grew till there would be as many as two thousand at a time, including many priests and religious—especially the Capuchins and Dominicans, the latter of whom sometimes sent their whole noviciate.

Custom allowed the visit to St. Peter's to be made the preceding evening. The pilgrims, therefore, on the morning of the day chosen proceeded individually to St Paul's, and there formed up into companies, and made their way along the via delle Sette Chiese to S. Sebastiano, saying the Rosary or the Litanies, or singing ' Laudi ' as they went. At S. Sebastiano Mass was said, and many received Holy Communion. When this was over it would be about noon, so they next went to a vineyard or garden, belonging to one of the Roman families who were friends of Philip's, for a picnic meal. Perhaps partly because the gardens of the Villa Mattei were conveniently close at hand, the church of S. Stefano Rotondo, on the Celian hill, was later substituted for the distant basilica of S. Sebastiano. In the garden of this, or of some other villa, they all sat on the grass and were served with bread and wine, an egg, cheese and some fruit ; during the meal there was instrumental music, but no loud talking which would dissipate the atmosphere of devotion. When this was ended the pilgrimage was resumed to the Lateran, S. Croce and S. Lorenzo, at each of which a sermon was preached, and finally St Mary Major, where the now tired pilgrims—the distance covered, if they went to S. Sebastiano, was about twelve miles—dispersed and made their way to their homes.

VII

THE pilgrimages to the Seven Churches, however, were to become the occasion of a heavy trial to Philip.

From the moment when he ascended the papal throne, in 1555, Paul IV had thrown himself heart and soul into the work of reform. Stern and imperious in character, he was no respecter of persons ; Cardinals who proved intractable were thrown into prison or banished from Rome ; decrees were published sending back to their dioceses bishops who lived in idleness about the court ; abuses were swept ruthlessly away. At the same time strong measures were taken to prevent the spread of heresy in Italy. The Inquisition was reorganized and its powers extended, and in 1558 the first Index of prohibited books was published.

The great tragedy of his life was the Pope's discovery, in 1559, that his nephew, Carlo Carafa, whom he had entrusted with the actual government of the Papal States, in order that he might be free to devote all his own energies to the reform of the Church, had been guilty of almost every conceivable crime and vice from homicide downwards. Without hesitation, that all the world might witness his own complete sincerity, he dealt as ruthlessly with his own relatives as he would have done with utter

strangers. Stripped of their dignities and posses-
sions, his nephews and the other unworthy members
of his family were driven from Rome and from the
States of the Church.

As usually happens in parallel conditions, the
innocent were involved with the guilty in the
general atmosphere of suspicion. Whether it was
that calumnies had been deliberately spread against
Philip and his followers, or whether the authorities
thought that they had genuine cause for uneasiness,
we can imagine the dismay at the Oratory when it
was learned, in the spring of 1557, that Philip
had been ordered to appear before Virgilio Rosario,
the Cardinal of Spoleto, who was the Pope's Vicar.
By Rosario Philip was severely rebuked as an
introducer of novelties and an ambitious man ;
worst of all, he was accused of forming a sect.
Finally, he was forbidden to continue the exercises
of the Oratory until fresh permission should be
given, or to go about Rome in company with
others, and was suspended from hearing confessions for a fortnight.

Philip at once submitted and professed his
willingness to obey in all things, though it meant,
as he must have seen with anguish, the doom of the
work that he had spent the six years of his priesthood in building up. But however much he might
forbid his young men to walk with him through the
streets, nothing could keep them from following
him at a distance. Meanwhile he prayed with
all his might and got others to pray, till one day
there appeared at the Oratory a strange priest,
wearing a coarse habit and a cord, who said that
he had come on behalf of some religious who had
had a revelation about the opposition to the exer-

cises. They were to have the Forty Hours Prayer and great fruit would follow ; the persecution would end in the establishment and increase of the work, and those who opposed it would be punished by God.

On May 22 the Cardinal Vicar, on his way to an audience with the Pope, was seized with a fit of apoplexy in one of the antechambers. He was carried to his own apartments, but was dead before he reached them.

After Rosario's death the Pope's attitude changed. He was at length convinced of Philip's innocence, and permitted the resumption of the exercises of the Oratory, and of the pilgrimages to the Seven Churches, even expressing his regret that he could not take part in them personally. As a further mark of his favour he sent Philip two of the painted candles that are presented to the Pope on Candlemas Day.

Philip would never allow a word to be said against Rosario, and at once silenced those who wanted to comment on the just judgements of God as instanced in his sudden death.

In the preceding year his friends the Dominicans at the Minerva had been in trouble. In this trouble they had the fullest sympathy of Philip, who had always retained the veneration for Fra Girolamo Savonarola that he had learned from the fathers at S. Marco in Florence ; and it was to be the occasion of an incident which made a great impression on all who knew Philip. For when the first Index of prohibited books was being drawn up the proposal was made that the works of Savonarola should be placed upon it. The Jesuits and the Augustinians worked hard to secure this condemnation.

The Dominicans were no less zealous in defence of the orthodoxy of the friar's writings, however indefensible his disobedience to the Pope might have been. There was one Dominican Cardinal on the commission for drawing up the Index, Michele Ghislieri, the future Pius V, on whose sympathy they could count, and for six months Ercolani, the prior of the Minerva and a particular friend of Philip's, almost killed himself with overwork in his efforts to avert the condemnation.

Finally the time came when everything that humanly could be done had been done, and prayer alone could avail to help their cause.

Accordingly, on the day when the final decision was to be given the Blessed Sacrament was exposed in a private chapel inside the convent of the Minerva, where a number of friends and sympathizers had gathered to pray, with Philip and Tarugi among them. Philip was kneeling in a corner of the chapel in prayer when it was noticed that something had happened to him. His eyes were open and fixed on the Blessed Sacrament, and he was smiling slightly, but his limbs were perfectly rigid and he was icy cold—the recognized phenomena of an ecstasy. They carried him into an adjoining room and laid him on a bed, where he remained for a considerable time. When he came to himself he exclaimed, ' Victory! Victory ! Our prayer has been heard.' And on their pressing him for an explanation he told the prior that the question had been settled in their favour, and at length revealed that he had seen Jesus Christ in the Sacred Host giving his blessing to all who were present.

In actual fact, at the very time of the vision it was being decided that a few of Savonarola's sermons should be placed on the Index—perhaps for the sake of saving faces—not because they were heretical, but because they were intemperate, while the rest of his works were considered not deserving of any kind of censure whatsoever.

Another thing that impressed people about Philip, though of quite another kind, was the extraordinary power he showed at the bedsides of the dying. Two striking instances occurred in the same year as the ecstasy just related.

The first case was that of Philip's confessor, Persiano Rosa. This good priest, in spite of his admirable life, seemed to be without the prospect of an easy or peaceful death. On the day preceding it he kept on sitting up and making the sign of the Cross, then throwing himself from one side of the bed to the other, as though in great terror. When Philip arrived Rosa greeted him with the words, ' Saint Philip, pray for me,' and then begged him to drive away a fierce black dog which was trying to tear him. Philip knelt down to pray, and told the others present to say a Pater and Ave for the dying man. He had scarcely started to pray when Rosa cried out : ' Thank God, the dog is going, the dog is running away. Look, he has reached the door ! ' Philip rose and sprinkled the dying man and the room with holy water, and his conflict was ended. The next day Rosa died peacefully.

A young man of eighteen named Gabriele Tana, one of Philip's earliest penitents, had to pass through a whole series of temptations before peace was granted him. First of all he was filled with an inordinate desire to live longer, but Philip told him he must make him a present of his will, which he would offer to God with the Host on the paten, as he was going to say Mass for him at S. Pietro in Montorio. When Philip returned Gabriele was in quite a different frame of mind, desiring only ' to be dissolved and to be with Christ,' and this continued all the next day. Before he left him that evening Philip foretold other temptations, and Salviati and Tarugi who stayed behind were to summon him if necessary.

Scarcely an hour had passed when Gabriele was tempted to presumption, thinking his salvation already secured through good works. Recognizing the temptation he repelled it, but then declared himself unable to utter the name of Jesus, though he pronounced it several times in order to state his inability. Philip was sent for, and when he arrived Gabriele was able to repeat the holy name several times to his own satisfaction. A temptation against faith followed next, and this too was vanquished by Philip's prayers, while the bystanders repeated the Credo aloud. Finally, he, too, was terrified by a vision of ' black dogs ' ; but Philip, placing his hands on Gabriele's head, rebuked the evil spirit, who at length departed leaving the boy in peace.

Everyone thought that he would have strength enough now to last till the next day, but Philip said, ' It will not be so ; the instant he moves from his present position he will die.' Half an hour afterwards he turned towards his right side, where Philip stood, and with the holy name on his lips died.

An almost similar case occurring three years later is interesting as giving us the words of one of the Oratory hymns. In this case it was a musician named Sebastiano who was dying. He, too, had terrifying visions, and was restored to peace by

Philip's cheerful presence, with his habitual ex-
clamation, ' Che c'è ? Che c'è ? ' (' What's all
this ? ') Finally he broke into one of the hymns he
had learned at the Oratory, beginning, ' Jesus,
Jesus, Jesus, let everyone call on Jesus,' and a little
later died in Philip's arms.

VIII

IN August 1559 Paul IV died. The conclave
met in September, but it was not until Christmas
Day that Cardinal Gian Angelo Medici, a Milanese,
was elected Pope and took the name of Pius IV.
In character he was the very antithesis of his pre-
decessor, for he was gentle and affable, while his
adroitness as a diplomat was concealed under an air
of simplicity. Yet the work of reform within the
Church was energetically carried on ; and the name
of Pius IV will always be honourably associated
with the triumphant termination of the Council of
Trent, and with the Creed in which the Church
once more explicitly formulated her faith.

In this pontificate, too, the vice of nepotism, the
evil custom long established by which successive
Popes advanced to high position the members
of their own families irrespective of their personal
character and merits, proved for once productive
of good. For in summoning from Arona to Rome his
nephew Charles Borromeo, and making him at the
age of twenty-two Cardinal Archbishop of Milan
and Secretary of State, Pius IV introduced into
the Sacred College not merely a worthy member—
other recent Popes had taken care to do this—but a
saint. His household was regulated like a religious

community, his life was retired and austere, and he allowed himself no recreations beyond the half religious, half literary ' Academies ' held on certain evenings at the Vatican. In every way he strove to exemplify in practice the decrees of the Council of Trent, whether in Rome, so long as he remained there, or in Milan, whither he returned, in obedience to the decrees of Trent binding bishops to residence in their dioceses, as soon as his uncle could spare him.

There is no record as to how Philip and Charles Borromeo, the one lively, humorous, at home with men of the world, the other dignified, studious, solemn, first became acquainted, but it seems likely that it was early in the pontificate. They appear together at the death-bed of Pius IV. At any rate, dissimilar as they were in character their zeal and supernatural spirit drew them together, and their correspondence after Charles Borromeo had returned to Milan shows that, in spite of certain misunderstandings, they remained firm friends. Personal contact was renewed on the occasions of the Cardinal's visits to Rome, and whenever for any reason his subjects were in Rome, they were always recommended to go to the Oratory and to make the acquaintance of Philip. There is frequent mention of Philip and the Oratory in the letters written to the Cardinal in Milan by Speciano, his agent in Rome, who lodged at S. Girolamo.

In 1562 there died in great peace Philip's devoted friend and penitent, who had proved also a good friend to the Dominicans at the Minerva in their trouble, Giambattista Salviati. Both Philip and the Dominican prior, Ercolani, were at his side.

In the next year it was Philip himself who was

almost at death's door, his illness being brought on by overwork.

For besides his constant work in the confessional and the daily meetings in the Oratory, as Philip's reputation grew with the miracles attributed to his prayers, he was more and more in demand on all sides. We have seen him at the bedsides of the dying ; but there were countless others to whom he was called in times of sickness, and whom he often cured by his vehement prayers, or by his touch ; and very often his presence brought relief in difficult cases of childbirth. Then, too, there were his expeditions by night to bring secret aid to those who would have been ashamed to accept alms given openly, and the days when he took his young men or boys to play games on the slopes of the Janiculum, near S. Onofrio. But—and this is typical of the intermingling of the two sides of Philip's life—he only used to start the game with them, and then, when it was well under way, he would withdraw, and taking a little book from his pocket containing the account of the Passion from the four Gospels, would begin to pray and weep. So ready was he to answer every call on him and to be at everyone's disposal, that one of his friends told him that he made himself too cheap. Philip's reply was : ' I tell you that those of my penitents who are most devout are those whom I gained by exposing myself at night to convert them.' This is in the same vein as his famous reply to those who complained that his young men made too much noise near his room, and disturbed the house : ' They may chop wood on my back,' he said, ' so long as they do not sin.'

But such a life took too great a toll of his constitution, and in 1563 he became seriously ill. The illness began with acute neuritis in the right arm accompanied by fever, and his condition became so serious that it was pronounced hopeless by three well-known doctors, who had done everything possible for him. But though he made a general confession and received the last sacraments so as to be completely prepared for death, he himself declared all along that he would not die this time. God, he said, had given him too many graces to let him die so little prepared to appear before Him as he then was—it was always a maxim of Philip's that ' spiritual persons ' may count on being warned by God when the hour of their death is approaching —and in three months he had completely recovered.

It must have been almost immediately after his recovery that he was approached by a deputation from the Florentine colony in Rome, with the request that he would take charge of their national church dedicated to S. John.

The present church of S. Giovanni dei Fiorentini, which stands on the banks of the Tiber only a short distance from the Ponte S. Angelo, was built for his countrymen by the Florentine Pope, Leo X, in 1519, and it was served by a community of from eight to ten priests who were responsible for all the spiritual ministrations connected with it. The superior of this community having recently died, it was now proposed that Philip should take his place, and that others of his followers should go to S. Giovanni with him. Philip asked for a few days to think the matter over, and eventually declined the invitation, because he was unwilling to leave S. Girolamo and his work there.

The Florentines, however, would not accept his

refusal ; and when three of their most influential representatives had failed to prevail on Philip to change his mind, they went to the Pope instead, and asked him to use his authority to make Philip accept the charge. Pius IV consented, and as soon as he understood that it was the Pope's will that he should take charge of S. Giovanni, Philip gave way, but on condition that he himself should be allowed to remain at S. Girolamo. Accordingly, while he continued to live where he had lived ever since his ordination, he had three of his disciples ordained— Cesare Baronio, Giovan Francesco Bordini and Alessandro Fedeli — and sent them to live at S. Giovanni.

In contrast with Baronius and Fedeli, who were true disciples of Philip, the second named, Bordini, a man of great talent who soon acquired a reputation as a brilliant preacher, eventually showed himself to have little of Philip's spirit. Not only was he a talker and full of self-assurance, he was ambitious and mixed himself up with the affairs of the Court, finally quitting Philip's Congregation on his appointment as Bishop of Cavaillon.

With these three at S. Giovanni dei Fiorentini there were two Florentine priests and a Spaniard who were not of Philip's circle, and there were soon added, though not yet priests, Francesco Maria Tarugi, of whom we have spoken, and Angelo Velli, a gentle and lovable character who was to be Philip's second successor in the government of the Congregation. The community was completed by two boys of about sixteen, Alessandro Fedeli's nephew, Germanico, and Ottavio Paravicini, Baronius' pupil, who eventually became a Cardinal. But besides these a number of young clerics and other ecclesiastics lived as boarders in the house, and were expected to observe the few simple rules which were drawn up to direct the daily life of the community.

Three times a day Philip's disciples went to S. Girolamo—in the morning to go to confession, in the afternoon to hear or to preach the sermons in the Oratory, and again in the evening for the half-hour of mental prayer. In the house at S. Giovanni they waited at table in turn, and for some while took it in turn to do the cooking. Baronius left the inscription in charcoal over the fireplace *Baronius Coquus Perpetuus* (Baronius the permanent cook). Germanico Fedeli and Ottavio Paravicini read week and week about during meals, but every day after the reading had lasted for about two-thirds of the meal it was stopped, and the rest of the time was spent in a discussion on some point of moral theology. On festivals besides hearing confessions and giving Communion they sang Mass, and Vespers too ; and the preachers wore in the pulpit the ample surplice specially dear to the Florentines in contrast with the short cotta of the Roman clergy. After Vespers they met Philip for the open-air Oratory, or the special festal exercises held indoors.

This record of their daily routine is extremely important in the history of Philip's work and the development of his Congregation, because it is the beginning of community life amongst priests of the Oratory as such. And we find already established, in addition to the daily attendance at the sermons and the evening mental prayer, not only the sung Mass and Vespers on feasts, which were later to be specifically ordained by the constitutions of the

Oratory, but also the peculiarly Oratorian custom of a theological discussion in the refectory at community meals.

Thus they continued for ten years. But at the end of that time, to save the priests at S. Giovanni the inconvenience of having to go every afternoon and again every evening to S. Girolamo, the Florentines built a more spacious Oratory at S. Giovanni, and thither the exercises were transferred in 1574. The impression produced by the exercises of the Oratory on Giovanni Giovenale Ancina at the time when they had only recently been transferred to S. Giovanni may be considered typical of that which they must have made on many young men. On May 20, 1576, he wrote to his brother, Giovanni Matteo :

' For some time past I have been going to the Oratory of S. Giovanni de' Fiorentini, where they deliver every day most beautiful spiritual discourses on the Gospel, or on the virtues and vices, or on ecclesiastical history, or the lives of the Saints. There are three or four who preach every day, and bishops, prelates, and other persons of distinction go to hear them. At the conclusion there is a little music to console and recreate the mind, which is fatigued by the preceding discourses. They have gone through the life of the glorious St Francis and those of his first disciples, and of St Antony of Padua. I assure you it is a most delightful exercise, and a most consoling and edifying thing ; and I regret very much that neither you nor I knew of this noble and holy practice last year.

' You must know, too, that those who deliver the discourses are men of distinction, in holy orders, and of most exemplary and spiritual life. Their superior is a certain Reverend Father Philip, an old man of sixty, but wonderful in many respects, and especially for holiness of life, and for his astonishing prudence and skill in inventing and promoting spiritual exercises ; he was the author of that great work of charity which was done at the Trinità de' Pellegrini during the last Jubilee. Fathers Toledo, Possevino and others report wonderful things of him. In fact, they say he is an oracle not only in Rome but in the distant parts of Italy, and in France and Spain, so that many come to him for counsel ; in a word, he is another Ruysbroek, or Thomas à Kempis or Tauler.'

This letter is worth quoting in full not only because it seems to retain all the warmth of the impression recently received, but also because it is the record of the widespread veneration in which Philip was already held. The writer of it, the Blessed John Juvenal Ancina, entered the Congregation of the Oratory in 1578, played an important part in the foundation of the Naples Oratory and, much against his will, was made Bishop of Saluzzo in 1602. He died two years later, and was beatified by Leo XIII in 1890. His brother, to whom the letter was written, also entered the Congregation, and died a member of it in 1630.

Yet in spite of the general favour with which the Oratory was regarded in Rome it still had its detractors, some of whom persisted in suggesting that it cloaked the formation of a new Lutheran sect, or at least that the laymen who sometimes spoke were guilty of imprudence if not of positive error. It was alleged, for instance, that the story of St Apollonia throwing herself into the fire had been related without its being made clear that she did so only by a particular inspiration of the Holy Ghost. These attacks continued for some years, and though the Cardinal Archbishop of Milan, St Charles, used all his influence in defence of the Oratory, in 1570 the suspicions of the sternly zealous St Pius V, who had succeeded Pius IV in 1566, were strongly aroused. He therefore charged two Dominican friars (he was himself a Dominican), independently of one another, to go and listen to the discourses at the Oratory, and to report on everything that was said and done there.

Their report when it was made was entirely favourable, and the Pope was satisfied. But the atmosphere of suspicion was galling to Philip, and he began to consider proposals made by St Charles of transferring the Oratory to Milan—even of going there himself. For the time being, however, nothing further came of the discussions.

In 1574 several Barnabites, or Clerks Regular of St Paul, a new religious Congregation founded in Milan by St Antonio Maria Zaccaria, were in Rome looking for a house and church in which to establish themselves in the city. They had the active sympathy and help of Philip in their quest, and in the meanwhile lodged near him at S. Girolamo and attended the evening exercises of the Oratory. In consequence of the intimate intercourse between Philip's disciples and these visitors, there was for a time some talk of their becoming Barnabites, a course which the Barnabites would have welcomed. Philip's reasons for ultimately rejecting the proposals for union were given in characteristic words which deserve consideration by all who have in contemplation a serious change in their state of life : ' It is a good thing to change from an evil life to a

good one ; but to change from a good state to a
better is a thing to be long and well considered.'
It was the Barnabite, Tito degli Alessi, who wrote of
Philip and his followers : 'All these priests show
him great submission and reverence, even though
sometimes he gives them some good mortifications ;
but he has a way of striking hard without wound-
ing.' So great was the Barnabites' opinion of his
discernment in the matter of vocations that their
General gave directions that no novices were to be
received in Rome unless they had been approved
by Philip.

One last threat to Philip's work was to prove the
occasion of the definitive establishment of the
Congregation of the Oratory. A certain ecclesiastic
had had to be expelled from the community at S.
Giovanni dei Fiorentini. In revenge for this he
spread such serious calumnies against Philip and
his disciples, and so stirred up against them the
feelings of the deputies who administered the church
of the Florentines, that they were on the point of
taking away from Philip the charge that they had
been so overwhelmingly persistent that he should
accept. One of their number, however, was strenu-
ous in his defence, and in the end his counsel
prevailed so that nothing was done. But it was this
incident that finally persuaded Philip that his work
was insecure so long as its existence was dependent
on the goodwill of such bodies as the deputies
governing S. Giovanni or S. Girolamo, and that,
in spite of any personal reluctance, he must obtain
for the Oratory a church and house of its own if he
would ensure its permanent survival.

Two churches amongst various that might have
been obtainable seemed well fitted for the purpose—

S. Maria in Monticelli, which had a good house for the community, and S. Maria in Vallicella, which was in a more central position. It was the Pope himself who eventually selected the latter, saying that it would be the more convenient for the court. Accordingly, by a bull of Gregory XIII ratified on July 15, 1575, there was erected in perpetuity in the church of S. Maria in Vallicella ' a Congregation of secular priests and clerics known as the Oratory,' and they were given authority to make such statutes and rules for the well-being of the Congregation as they should think fit, provided that they were not in contravention of the decrees of the Council of Trent, and subject to approval by the Apostolic See.

IX

PHILIP'S APOSTOLATE

BEFORE carrying the story of Philip's life and the development of his Congregation further, it would be an advantage if we could gain some more general view of the principles of Philip's apostolate, of the spirit which directed it, and of his methods of dealing with men and women. But the truth would seem to be that his method was, in effect, to have no standardized method. He acted from day to day and from hour to hour according to the impulses of tender charity which moved him to treat one soul in this way and another in that, in obedience to the interior movements of the Holy Spirit, whose guidance he so humbly and constantly sought and so faithfully tried to follow. He won souls partly by his personal charm, partly by the exercise of supernatural gifts. He prayed and trembled and wept ; he read comic books and went into ecstasies ; he caressed young men and boxed their ears to make them cheerful ; he made jokes and told men all their sins before they confessed them. No one knew what he would do next ; but there were few who could resist the charm of Philip's personality and the vehemence of Philip's prayers combined.

The only way, therefore, to complete our picture would seem to be to give some concrete examples of the way in which he used these natural and supernatural gifts to gain souls to Christ, in addition to those which have already occurred, and then to attempt to gather from his own practice and from the advice he gave—often in quaint form—to others, the characteristic spirit of Philip's school of perfection.

The name of Marcello Ferro occurs frequently in the accounts of Philip's life, as the instrument by which many were brought under his influence, and as a devoted disciple. The story of his own conversion is typical.

Marcello belonged to a distinguished Roman family, and though he was a cleric holding a rich benefice, he dressed in coloured clothes like a layman, and thought a great deal about them. He was in the cloister of the Minerva one year on the eve of the feast of St Dominic, when he met a young man who was a penitent of Philip's. In the course of conversation the young man said to him : ' A priest from S. Girolamo named Philip is in the habit of coming here to Vespers and Compline. If only you could speak to him, what a happy thing it would be for you ! ' Marcello begged to be introduced, and had scarcely done so when Philip entered the church with Salviati and several others. Marcello followed them and saw Philip kneel down, cover his face with his hands, and begin to weep and tremble. After Compline, during the whole of which Philip had continued to tremble, Marcello had a long conversation with him, and was invited to S. Girolamo to hear the sermons.

He accepted the invitation, and went to the exercises at the Oratory for four or five days, after which he made a general confession. During his confession Philip, trembling all the time, kept his eyes raised towards heaven, and revealed to Marcello all his sins. Before giving him absolution he said : ' My son, do not resist the Holy Ghost ; God wishes to save you.' Marcello went on going to see Philip every day, and though he still dressed like a layman Philip said never a word. By the end of a fortnight he was ashamed of his secular clothes and gave them up of his own accord. It was a sign that his conversion was completed.

Francesco Zazzara was working very hard studying law. He was a young man with ambitions. One day Philip called him, and Francesco went and knelt at his feet while Philip, caressing him as he spoke, began to voice aloud all the young man's hopes and plans. ' How happy you are,' he said, ' now you are studying; after a while you will get your doctorate, and begin to make money and advance your family ; you will become an advocate, and one day, perhaps, attain to the highest positions in your profession.' This was exactly what Francesco had been thinking to himself, and he let Philip run on quite contentedly. But suddenly the recital stopped, and Philip, bending forward, whispered in his ear, ' And then ? ' Even when he got home Francesco could not shake off the impression that the words, and the way in which they were spoken, had made on him. He was studying ; he was getting on well and had prospects of getting on better still— and then ? Where was it all leading ? Eventually he abandoned his career in the world to enter Philip's Congregation, and persevered in it till he died in the year of Philip's canonization.

Philip had a particular detestation of avarice, and a very poor opinion of those who showed any propensity to what he called ' the pest of the soul.' When a man he suspected of being avaricious asked for leave to fast, or perform some corporal penance, he would say, ' No, give alms ' ; and one of his frequently repeated sayings was, ' Let the young beware of the sins of the flesh and the old of avarice, and then we shall all be saints.' Priests were warned that, if they wished to gain souls, they must leave purses alone, and that they must on no account meddle in the matter of wills, because this always raises suspicions in the minds of other people. ' Give me ten truly detached men,' he used to say, ' and I will convert the world with them.'

Giovan Tommaso Arena used to go to the exercises at the Oratory just to make fun of them. The other young men were very indignant, and tried to get Philip to have him ejected, but they were merely told to be patient. Nor would he allow a word to be said, although the same kind of thing went on for a considerable while. In the end Philip's patience succeeded where any kind of rebuke would almost certainly have failed. Giovan Tommaso entered the Dominican Order, and made a good death while he was still a novice.

Pietro Focile was a facetious young man, who came to the Oratory one day in a fantastic costume. Philip's eye was fixed upon him all through the exercises, and by the end of the afternoon Pietro was conscious that an extraordinary change had come over him, a change that was noticed even by his friends. After a week had passed he resolved to make a good confession, and went and knelt by Philip's confessional. But Philip, having heard some other confessions, told Pietro that he could not hear him then, and that he must come back some other time. Every time he came he was treated in the same way, but the more Philip put him off, the more anxious Pietro became to be disburdened of his sins. At last the day came when he was allowed to make his confession, to his great joy, and afterwards he remained firmly devoted to Philip.

Innumerable instances are given of Philip's revealing to penitents concealed, or even forgotten sins. Rafaelle Lupo, for example, whose life was not of the best, was taken by a friend to hear the sermons at S. Girolamo. Afterwards, in the hope of doing him good, this friend took him to Philip's room and introduced him as a young man who was going to come regularly to the sermons, and wished to begin by making a good confession. Rafaelle was extremely indignant, as he had neither expressed, nor even formed, any such intention ; but rather than be openly rude he knelt down and made a false confession. At the conclusion of it Philip pressed the young man's head to his heart and said : ' The Holy Spirit has revealed to me that there is not a word of truth in all you have said.' Taken completely by surprise, the young man was genuinely moved to sorrow and made a general confession of his whole life. Acting on Philip's advice he eventually became a Franciscan friar.

Philip often declared, and many testified to his having proved it to themselves, that he could detect the guilt of impurity in others by their stench. This extraordinary sensitiveness may be attributed to the fact, revealed in confidence to a penitent by way of encouragement, that he himself had always preserved his chastity intact. This so eminent degree of virtue may in itself constitute, in part at least, the secret of that indefinable quality about him which enabled him ' to draw souls as the magnet draws iron,' and gave his eyes a brightness which no painter could ever succeed in reproducing. In this

connection a description of Philip given in a letter
by Giovenale Ancina may be quoted : ' He is a
beautiful old man, white as an ermine ; his flesh
is soft and exquisitely pure, so that if he holds his
hand against the light, it seems as transparent as
alabaster.' Other manifestations of this extreme
sensibility were his fastidiousness about the cleanness
of his clothes, however poor and patched they might
be, and his repugnance to drinking from a coarse
glass, or using a chalice used by other priests—a
repugnance he set himself deliberately to overcome.

Once a young man omitted in his confession a
grave sin because he was ashamed, but at the end
of it Philip said : ' You have not come here in
sincerity ; you have omitted such and such sins,'
mentioning the precise circumstances. Yet another
youth, having committed a very grave sin, went to
confession, but when he tried to put it into words
found himself simply unable to speak. Philip,
therefore, took pity on him and said : ' Do not be
afraid ; I will tell you your sin,' and he proceeded
to relate it exactly as it had happened.

A curious incident reveals Philip's supernatural
insight in a different way. A young man of about
sixteen came to S. Girolamo dressed like a layman,
but Philip fixed his eyes on him and said : ' Tell
me the truth, are you not a priest ? ' The boy
admitted that he was, and explained that he had
been forced by his relations to be ordained, in
order that they might succeed to some property.
Philip afterwards told Tarugi that he knew him to
be a priest by the splendour of the sacerdotal
character which shone on his forehead.

Another incident illustrates both an extraordinary
knowledge on Philip's part, and his power by a few

words to dispel temptations or scruples. A certain nun at S. Marta was going to tell him at the grill a temptation that she had never mentioned to anyone ; she was obsessed by the thought that she would be lost. But as soon as he saw her, before she had said a word, Philip said : ' What are you doing, Scholastica, what are you doing ? Paradise is yours.' ' No, father,' she replied, ' I am afraid it will be otherwise ; for it seems to me I shall be lost.' ' No,' said Philip, ' I tell you that Paradise is yours, and I will prove it to you. Tell me, for whom did Christ die ? ' ' For sinners.' ' Well,' asked Philip, ' and what are you ? ' ' A sinner.' ' Then,' he concluded, ' Paradise is yours, because you repent of your sins,' and these words completely delivered her from her temptation.

But though his ways were generally so gentle, if other methods were necessary he was well able to use them. Being once summoned to a criminal under sentence of death who was obstinately resisting all attempts to bring him to a proper frame of mind, Philip seized him by the collar and laid him out flat on the ground. The response to this treatment was immediate. He made his confession, and met death in excellent dispositions. In another case, where a young man seemed impervious to both appeals and rebukes, Philip finally said to him : ' Well, I see we must come to facts with you,' and making him kneel down with his head on his knees he said : ' Look, now, with your own eyes at the pains which await you in hell ! ' The youth, having remained with his head on Philip's knees for a short while, began to show signs of intense agitation, and was soon induced to make a good confession. An example of successful ' suggestion,' moderns would say. Suggestion—perhaps ; that it was successful is quite clear.

In many cases Philip's persuasiveness, and the power of his prayers, succeeded in converting Jews to the faith. Marcello Ferro fell in with two young Jews in the portico of St Peter's one year on the eve of the feast of SS. Peter and Paul, and took them to S. Girolamo. So much were they taken with Philip that for some months they went to see him nearly every day. When these visits suddenly ceased, Marcello was sent to their house to discover the cause, and found that one of them was seriously ill. The mother took Marcello upstairs to see him, and though he had been refusing all food, he would take whatever his visitor offered him. When Marcello whispered that Father Philip wished to be remembered to him, he was greatly pleased, so before leaving Marcello said : 'Remember that you have promised Father Philip that you will become a Christian.' ' I do remember it,' the Jew replied, ' and intend to do so if God spares my life.' The incident was reported to Philip who said : ' Do not be afraid. We will help him with our prayers and he will be converted.' The Jew recovered, and returned to Philip with his brother, and both became Christians.

Gregory XIII himself expressed a doubt about the wisdom of leaving with his family another Jew who had recently been won by Philip to the faith, lest it should imperil his perseverance, but Philip said that he was confident that the father would be converted through the son. This actually happened; and some years later this man sent four young nephews of his, who had lost their father, to the Vallicella to be instructed. For some while Philip never directly discussed the question of religion with them, but one evening he told them to beg the God of Abraham, Isaac and Jacob to inspire them with the knowledge of the truth ; he had already made the same prayer himself, and would do holy violence to God next morning at Mass. While Philip was saying Mass next day a quite unexpected change came over the four brothers, and they expressed their willingness to become Christians. If the genuineness of so sudden a conversion is questioned, the equally sudden conversion of Alphonse Ratisbonne, which occurred in the middle of the last century, may be quoted as a parallel.

Philip also obtained by his prayers at Mass the sudden cure of one of the four brothers, who had become dangerously ill during the period of their instruction. He said that he feared that if he died the Jews would say that the Christians had killed him.

Although Philip is always counted as one of the leading figures in the movement generally spoken of as the Counter-Reformation, living as he did practically all his life in Rome, he rarely came into actual contact with any of those who had adopted the ' new religion.' There was, however, the case of Lavinia della Rovere, a member of the same family as Pope Julius II, who had adopted unorthodox opinions under the influence of a friend, and whom he brought back to being a devout practising Catholic ; and there was the more famous case of Paleologus.

This man, who had been condemned by the Inquisition as an obstinate heretic, was actually being led out to die in the Campo de' Fiori when Philip, pushing his way through the crowd, embraced the poor man, and began to appeal to him with such tenderness and fervour that he showed signs of yielding. The respect in which Philip was held sufficed to suspend proceedings while an order was obtained from the Pope—it was Gregory XIII, who greatly venerated Philip—that the sentence should not be carried out. The procession returned to the prison, and Philip continued to visit the prisoner almost every day. He brought him the lives of the Blessed Giovanni Colombini and the Blessed Jacopone da Todi—favourite books of his own— to read, because he thought that the intellectual pride that is the cause of error is more effectively overcome by the examples of the Saints, and by simple books, than by argumentation. Unhappily, in this case his labour was unfruitful. Two years later, after various fluctuations, Paleologus suffered death as a relapsed heretic ; but he was assisted on the scaffold by Tarugi and Bordini, and at the last gave signs of contrition.

There is one interesting link between Philip and the persecuted English Catholics of Queen Eliza- beth's reign. The English College, founded by Gregory XIII, occupied, and still occupies, a site in the via di Monserrato directly opposite S. Giro- lamo della Carità. Philip must, therefore, have been constantly meeting the young students of the college, and he used to greet them with the words of the hymn in the Office of the Holy Innocents: *Salvete Flores Martyrum* (' Hail, flowers of the Martyrs '). There is a tradition that they always went to get Philip's blessing before setting out for their own country as priests, with the certainty of having to face a dreadful martyrdom should they fall into the hands of Elizabeth's Government ; but one who neglected, out of contempt, to get this blessing, ended by falling away from the faith.

X

PRAYER : MORTIFICATION : THE SPIRIT OF JOY

PHILIP'S methods always allowed human
affection full play ; Fabrizio de' Massimi,
who knew him so well, afterwards testified of him :
' He was so affectionate that he drew all the world
after him in the most wonderful way imaginable.'
But it was never merely human ; it was poured out
on all souls alike, that he might gain all ; it was the
effect of his desire to kindle in others the fire of
the love of God with which he himself burned, a fire
kept alive within himself by his unceasing prayer.

So intense was his prayer that it was sometimes
necessary to distract him of set purpose in the
afternoon for the sake of his health, or to enable him
to sleep at night. Those who came suddenly into
his room would find him so absorbed that he never
noticed their presence—this happened once with
Fabrizio de' Massimi—and if he visited a church he
scarcely dared to kneel down for more than a
moment, for fear he should be completely carried
away. This would sometimes happen to him in the
presence of other people, and even out of doors.
And once, on the occasion of an audience, he got
close up to the Pope without noticing he was there,
or uncovering his head. An experience of this nature
in the pulpit, when he had to break off his sermon
and come down because he felt himself being carried
away, made him resolve to preach no more in

public. He found it difficult even to say his Office for the same reason, unless he had someone to recite it with him, though he always tried to say every word with the greatest care, and would never, if he was well, avail himself of the privilege, granted him in his old age by Gregory XIV, of saying the Rosary instead.

But in spite of this exceptional faculty of recollection at all times—and he used to say that a man who cannot pray directly after dinner looks as though he has not got the spirit of prayer at all—he had his set times, and even special places for prayer. For both at S. Girolamo, and afterwards at the Vallicella, he had a little loggia constructed up on the roof (a kind of open gallery, a common architectural feature in Italy) from which he could see the sky and the open country, and thither he liked to retire morning and evening to pray. He would sometimes spend several hours there, but if he was wanted he always came down at once because this, he said, was ' leaving Christ for Christ,' and caused him no distraction from his prayer. On winter evenings he would pray for two or three hours before his crucifix, with a little lamp so arranged as to throw a light only on the figure. Before he went to sleep he placed at the head of his bed a watch, his beads and a figure of Our Lord detached from the cross, so that he could begin to pray directly he awoke. He did not ordinarily sleep for more than four or five hours, and if he had been hindered from praying during the day he subtracted the time from his rest. If others told him he allowed himself too little sleep he would reply : ' Paradise is not made for sluggards,' or something of the sort.

Proportionate to his love of prayer was his confidence in obtaining anything he prayed for, and his zeal to lead others to practise mental prayer. ' The man without prayer,' he used to say, ' is like an animal without reason.' Yet—and this is noteworthy—although one case is recorded in which he taught a woman to meditate clause by clause on the Our Father, he was very reluctant to give any detailed direction with regard to methods of mental prayer, and warned confessors not to try to impose their own methods and exercises on penitents, but to leave them free to follow the drawings of the Holy Ghost. A penitent, for instance, who asked Philip to teach him how to make mental prayer was told : ' Be humble and obedient and the Holy Ghost will teach you.' In the same way, though he recommended beginners to meditate on the Four Last Things, he seems to have been averse from giving ' points ' for meditation, or prescribing particular subjects. Everyone, he said, should follow the particular attraction that God gives him in prayer, and when he draws us to meditate on one mystery we should not go on trying to meditate on another. Philip's ideas would thus seem to be in harmony rather with the more ancient tradition with regard to mental prayer than with the school of spirituality that was then beginning to come into prominence.

He always attached great importance to spiritual reading, and it was a saying of his that, both for study and for prayer, we should read chiefly ' the authors whose names begin with S '—that is, the lives and writings of the Saints. All alike were recommended to practise ejaculatory prayer, but particularly those who were not capable of formal meditation. Some of his own favourite ejaculations

were, ' Deus in adjutorium meum intende, Domine
ad adjuvandum me festina,' ' My Jesus, if thou
uphold me not I shall fall,' ' I would fain love thee,
my Jesus, but I know not how,' ' I distrust myself,
but I trust in thee, my Jesus,' ' Virgin Mary
Mother of God, pray to Jesus for me,' or simply,
' Virgin and Mother.' One or other of these ejaculations he used to recommend people to say in the
form of a rosary, instead of the Paters and Aves.

On one point Philip was quite explicit—the
absolute necessity for humility, detachment and
mortification if anyone wishes to acquire the spirit
of prayer, or to make any progress in the spiritual
life. ' To desire to give ourselves to prayer without
mortification,' he used to say, ' is like a bird trying
to fly before it is fledged.'

On his own part, while all Rome venerated him
as a saint, consulted him as an oracle, and almost
ceased to wonder at his miracles, Philip seemed to be
scarcely tempted to vainglory, because he was
genuinely unable to see any kind of good in himself.
His only preparation for Mass was to protest that
he would do every manner of evil if God did not
uphold him ; in his illnesses he always promised
God that if he got well again he would begin to do
good, while to young people he used to say :
' O happy you who have time to do good, which I
have never done.' If there appeared to be any good
in him it was due to something or someone else :
to the Dominicans he used to say that any good in
him was due to the influence of the friars at S. Marco,
in Florence, when he was a boy, and to the Jesuits
that all he knew about mental prayer he had learned
from St Ignatius ; if the chapel shook with his
ecstatic trembling at Mass it was caused by the

prayers of an old woman kneeling close by ; if he cured someone miraculously it was to be attributed to the virtue of a reliquary.

Two stories illustrate Philip's humour, as well as his humble opinion of himself. A prelate one day found him moved to tears over the life of a saint he was reading, and on asking him why he wept received the answer : ' What ! and may I not weep, a poor orphan without father or mother ? ' Another day his doctor found him in tears over a book and asked him the reason. ' Because,' he said, ' this Saint, whose life I am reading, left the world to serve God, and I have never done any good, and everyone is better than I. Oh, Angelo ! ' he went on, ' if you were one day to see me whipped through the streets you would say, " Ah ! look at that fellow Philip who pretended to be so spiritual, give it him well." '

His gift of tears was itself no matter for pride. ' Even women from the streets are easily reduced to tears if you speak to them of God,' he said. As for his ecstasies, not only did he think nothing of them in his own case, but he was always positively suspicious of others who were subject to them. This was shown by his treatment of the Venerable Orsola Benincasa, whom he seemed still to be uncertain of, although she stood so well all the very severe tests of humility to which he subjected her, as a member of the commission appointed to examine the spirit of the visionary by Gregory XIII. Consulted about another nun who had frequent visions, he said she was to be told that when such apparitions came she must spit in their faces and make no account of them. And one day when Bordini had spoken of ecstasies in a sermon, Philip mounted the pulpit directly he came down, and said that he wished to add a word or two. ' I know,' he said, ' a woman of holy life who had continual ecstasies for a long time, and then God took them away from her. Now when do you think I esteemed that woman most, when she had ecstasies or when she had none ? I tell you that to my mind she was without comparison more to be esteemed when she had not ecstasies than when she had.'

But it was not only that Philip had a humble opinion of himself. According to him there are four steps in humility : ' To despise the world, to despise no man, to despise oneself and to despise being despised,' and he held that a man who cannot endure the loss of his honour is incapable of progress in the spiritual life. Consequently, although he had too much good sense, as well as too much sanctity, to undervalue corporal mortifications, they hold a place in Philip's life that is relatively small compared with the place they hold in the lives of some other saints, while, on the other hand, he went to really extraordinary lengths to try to court contempt, and make others despise him. In the same way, though he always warned young men against pampering their bodies, he was cautious lest they should attempt too much in the way of corporal penances. It is better, he held, in general to give the body too much food than too little, because it is easy to diminish the quantity, while if the constitution is once seriously impaired it is not so easily set up again. Yet, in the spiritual mortifications he inflicted on his penitents and disciples, with the object of destroying every vestige of pride, root and branch, he was relentless and uncompromising.

Perhaps one of the best illustrations of Philip's

ideas on the subject of mortification is to be found
in the case of Alberto the carpenter. This good man
asked Philip's leave to wear a hair shirt, and
received the reply : ' By all means, but on condition you wear it outside your coat.' He obeyed, and
continued wearing it—outside his coat—till his
death, winning for himself the nickname of ' Berto
of the hair shirt.' The all-important thing, Philip
always insisted, is the mortification of the *razionale*,
the reasoning faculty, the inclination to demand
the reason why about everything. This he sometimes expressed by saying : ' A man's sanctity lies
within the breadth of three fingers '—the breadth,
that is, of the forehead.

He had endless devices for making himself look
ridiculous and contemptible. We have pictures of
him receiving distinguished guests in his room
wearing a very small red beretta perched on the
top of his head, a red woollen garment down to his
knees outside his cassock, and a large pair of white
shoes ; or walking through the streets with half his
beard cut off, having himself shaved in public,
jumping about outside the church of S. Pietro in
Vincoli when there was a large concourse of people
for the feast in August, strutting about as though
to show off a fur cloak, or sniffing a big bunch of
broom flowers. One day, meeting his great friend
the Capuchin lay-brother, St Felix of Cantalice,
at his suggestion he took a long drink out of the
bottle the friar carried round his neck. In order to
return the mortification, Philip put his own priest's
hat on the friar's head. On another occasion,
being asked out to dine with a Cardinal, he took
with him a little earthenware dish of lentils.

Most useful of all in this way were his books of

jokes, which used to be produced or referred to for the benefit of those who came to call on him for the sake of seeing a saint. Four Polish noblemen were sent for this purpose by Clement VIII, but directly he heard them arriving Philip told Fr. Consolini to begin reading one of these books, and when his visitors entered the room they were asked to be good enough to wait till the story was finished. Fr. Consolini had to go on with the reading while Philip kept saying, ' You see what capital books I keep, and what important matters I have read to me ! ' The Poles took their leave, we learn, completely bewildered. On a visit to the wife of the Spanish Ambassador he appealed to Fr. Antonio Gallonio, who was with him, to confirm his assertion that he delighted in the beautiful books of poetry and tales he kept at home. But the reply was not the one he wanted : ' Why yes, Father, but what wonder when you cannot in any other way cool the fire of your love of God ? ' We can imagine what Gallonio got when they reached home : ' There, now, a pretty answer you gave me ! God forgive you ! What can you have been thinking of to say a thing like that ! '

His penitents and his subjects in the Congregation had to submit to mortifications of the same kind that he inflicted on himself, so that one day Fr. Niccolò Gigli said that he had no honour left, because Father Philip had taken it all away. Philip himself used to say that if any father thought himself better than ' those poor priests who go about with greasy breviaries under their arms, following the dead at funerals,' then he had not the spirit of the Congregation. Yet Philip never worked by hard and fast rules, and while some were mortified incessantly others never had to suffer the public humiliations that he was so ingenious in inventing.

A young man who appeared vain about a new suit of clothes was one day sent to take his place amongst the beggars outside St Mary Major's, and told to eat nothing that day but what he could get in alms ; and others were often told to beg at sermons, which was considered particularly degrading. He had a number of pairs of spectacles which he put on young men's noses before sending them on errands ; one youth was sent to ring a bell along a busy street, while another had to go about with a placard on his back which read : ' For having eaten curds and whey.' Another penitent was sent to have his hair cut by Philip's Capuchin friend, and St Felix, by arrangement with Philip, shaved the whole of his head. The use Philip made of his cat and dog as instruments of penance has already been told.

Nor were even such as Anna Borromeo, the sister of the Cardinal of Milan, exempt from such trials. This lady, who was pious but exaggeratedly scrupulous, once approached Philip's confessional a second time in the same day, whereupon he drove her away without hearing her confession, rebuking her in a loud voice before several other people. It was Philip's advice that confessors should as a rule be rather severe with women ; but he was not always so with Anna Borromeo, who was most devoted to him. She was married to Fabrizio Colonna, the son of the victor of Lepanto, and was in great distress when, after several years of married life, she had borne him no heir. When she confided in Philip he consoled her with the assurance that she would have two sons, and the prediction proved true.

The members of Philip's Congregation suffered even more severely than others if he thought there was any danger of their being tempted to pride. Fr. Antonio Gallonio not only had to wear a fur cloak through three summer months, but knowing a few songs in the patois of Norcia, he used frequently to be made to sing them in the presence of cardinals, and even of nuns. One poor lay-brother used regularly to be made to dance in the refectory in the presence of distinguished guests. Fathers of the Congregation were often sent out without cloaks, or in torn habits with holes in them. A kind gentleman, meeting one of the fathers looking particularly shabby, offered him a pair of sleeves as an alms. He refused the gift, but when Philip heard of it he sent him back to the gentleman to say that after all he would be very glad to accept the sleeves, as he was really in want of them.

Sometimes a preacher in the full fervour of his discourse would be told to hold his tongue and come down because Philip himself wished to speak, and many had to preach at a moment's notice. But perhaps the bitterest mortification in this way was reserved for Fr. Agostino Manni, who, having one day preached a particularly beautiful sermon, was ordered to deliver the same discourse six times running, without wilfully changing a single word, so that people who saw him mounting the pulpit began to say : ' Here comes the father who has only got one sermon.' And picture Tarugi's misery on being suddenly told that he must leave the Congregation, because he was unworthy to remain in it a day longer. He employed many other fathers to intercede for him, and offered to do any kind of penance if he was told his fault, but for days

Philip appeared inflexible. Then suddenly he forgave him, but said that he must never behave like that again. Tarugi was never told what he was supposed to have done.

Yet in spite of these mortifications—or rather, perhaps, as the fruit of the humility and simplicity that they produced—joy and cheerfulness have always been recognised as the distinguishing mark of Philip's school. In his own lifetime his room came to be known as ' the School of Christian Mirth ' ; and when his friend, Cardinal Valiero, wrote a dialogue in the platonic manner, in which Philip and various of his friends are represented as taking part in a discussion at a banquet, the title he gave it was ' Philip, or Christian Joy.' And years later, when Goethe during his travels in Italy came to know of Philip, he, too, felt impelled to write about him, and wrote of him as ' The Humorous Saint.' It was not only that no one ever saw Philip depressed or gloomy himself ; he could not bear to see anyone else sad. ' I will have no melancholy, no low spirits in my house,' he used to say ; though at the same time he used to warn people that mere buffoonery not only prevents spiritual progress but effectively roots out any spirituality we may have. He always liked cheerful people the best, because he said they are the more easily led to perfection.

One day, for example, two Capuchins, the one old and the other young, came to visit him, and the younger was bad-mannered enough to spit in his room. Philip pretended to fly into a violent rage, abused him roundly, and finally told him to take off his habit because he was no longer worthy to wear it. The older friar looked greatly shocked by this display, but the young one showed imperturbable good-humour and patience throughout, so that Philip at length embraced him saying, ' My son, persevere in this cheerfulness, for this is the true way to make progress in virtue.'

If he saw anyone looking sad he would sometimes give him a box on the ear, saying that it was not them but the devil he was beating. Everyone knew that a word from Philip, or a touch of his hand, was enough to cure the worst fit of depression, and Fabrizio de' Massimi found that just to stand near the door of Philip's room could restore his cheerfulness. There is a delightful simplicity, too, in the story of how he one day cured a father of the Congregation who was suffering from a fit of extreme depression, by only saying to him, ' Come now, let us run together.'

Perhaps it is this quality that makes certain saints like Philip, or Teresa of Avila, so ' actual ' to us now, in a way in which great men or women who were their contemporaries are not 'actual' to us. Since joy is one of the ' fruits of the Spirit ' it must have been present in the souls of all the saints ; but in certain of them at least it was concealed and restrained, while in the case of others—and pre-eminently in Philip—it was wholly unconcealed, and diffused itself over all who came into contact with them ; and it still seems to have the power to do as much.

XI

WHEN the church of S. Maria in Vallicella
was made over to Philip and his community,
the parish priest resigned his cure of souls, though a
pension from the parochial revenues was reserved
to him for life. Fr. Giovanni Antonio Lucci was
sent to take charge of the parish, and with him
went Germanico Fedeli, not yet a priest.

The church itself was very small, dark and half
buried in the ground. There was at first some
thought of restoring it, but it was soon found to be
in so ruinous a condition that their architect reported that the better course would be to pull it
down and build a new church. There was naturally
some hesitation at undertaking a work of this magnitude, particularly since they were without funds ;
but Philip, nothing daunted by any such consideration, one morning suddenly gave orders for the work
of demolition to be begun, and for plans for a new
church on a more splendid scale to be prepared.
Matteo di Castello, a well-known architect of the
time, was engaged, and gave his services gratuit-
ously.

On the morning when he was proposing to mark
out the plan of the new building a message came
from Philip, who was just going to say Mass at

S. Girolamo, to say that he wished to be present, and that they must wait till he came. When he arrived the architect carried the line as far as he thought suitable and stopped, but was told by Philip to carry it further. Twice more he was told to carry it further, and further still. Beginning to dig at the point that finally satisfied Philip they came upon an ancient wall, which served as a foundation for the whole of one side of the church, and provided materials for the rest of the foundations. The building was begun on September 17, 1575, only two months after the Vallicella had been handed over to Philip's Congregation, and the first stone was solemnly laid by Alessandro de' Medici, Archbishop of Florence and ambassador of the Grand Duke, who was later to become Leo XI.

The work advanced rapidly, Philip saying that he had made a bargain with the Madonna not to die before the church should be roofed in, and this in spite of the fact that when they started they had practically no funds at all. But by degrees contributions began to flow in, the pence of the poor, rings that women took from their fingers to give, and some liberal contributions by the rich. St Charles Borromeo had already given them 400 crowns for the erection of an Oratory, and promised recommendations to possible benefactors, and one of the first to contribute was Gregory XIII, who gave 8000 crowns in all at different times. In recognition of his generosity St Gregory the Great was joined with Our Lady as titular of the new church.

Fr. Antonio Lucci, who had been sent in the first place to take charge of the parish, and had been joined in 1576 by Baronius and Tarugi, was responsible also for superintending the building operations. This made him and his companion, Germanico Fedeli, unpopular with those in the neighbourhood who did not welcome the new building, and they went so far as to throw stones, and even to shoot at the fathers. On the other hand, he had signs of a supernatural protection. For during the demolition of the old church one corner was left standing to form a chapel for the Blessed Sacrament, with an ancient image of the Madonna, and one day Philip sent for him and told him to have the roof of this chapel taken down at once, because the night before he had seen the Madonna supporting it with her hand when it would otherwise have fallen. He went back, and when the workmen went to remove the roof it was found that the principal beam had in fact come out of the wall, and was suspended without visible support in the air.

By February 1577 the great nave of the church had been completed, and it was at once brought into use. The first Mass was sung by the Archbishop of Florence, Alessandro de' Medici, on February 3, Septuagesima Sunday, and the Pope granted a plenary indulgence to all who visited the church that day. A great crowd was attracted to the Lent sermons this same year by a Spanish Capuchin who was a moving orator. In the following April the exercises of the Oratory were transferred to the Vallicella, and in the course of the year, some neighbouring houses having been bought, the general move of the Congregation took place, and their connection with S. Giovanni de' Fiorentini was severed, though it was to be resumed for a short period at a subsequent date. By 1578 all were assembled in their new home—all, that is, with the

exception of Philip, who still clung to his rooms at
S. Girolamo.

About this time many new members were
attracted to the Congregation, including Antonio
Gallonio, Philip's earliest biographer, Agostino
Manni, Flaminio Ricci, Tommaso Bozio, a theological and historical writer, and the two Ancina
brothers, the Blessed Giovanni Giovenale and his
brother, Giovanni Matteo : the chief difficulty was
to find means to support, and room to house all the
vocations that presented themselves. Nor was it only
that their quarters were cramped ; on the scale on
which the church had been planned, it would be
necessary to pull down the houses in which the
fathers were then living before the transepts and
choir could be built. It is not surprising, therefore,
that when the neighbouring monastery of St Elizabeth fell vacant the fathers at once entered into
negotiations for its purchase, although Philip was
strongly opposed to incurring any additional debt.
In the end it was bought by Cardinal Pierdonato
Cesi, and in 1592 was given by him to the fathers,
together with another house.

In the following year the Cardinal did the Congregation a service of another kind, for it was he
who, at the fathers' request, obtained from the
Pope a command that Philip should leave S. Girolamo and go to live with the Congregation he had
founded at the Vallicella. Philip, of course, obeyed
at once ; but he made his removal an occasion
for a mortification of the kind he most loved. For
on St Cecilia's day, 1583, his friends had to march
with him from S. Girolamo to his new home in
solemn procession, carrying on their backs his pots
and pans and all his household goods, while the

prisoners in a gaol they had to pass looked out and jeered at them. Nor did his removal alter his manner of life in any degree ; for at the Vallicella he chose rooms in a remote part of the house, and had another loggia constructed on the roof where he could pray in solitude, beneath the open sky. The community was naturally delighted to have him in its midst, and consulted him on every point of moment as it had always done, but he took little part in its daily life, rarely appearing even in the refectory.

Cardinal Cesi had now determined to become the benefactor of Philip's Congregation on a grand scale, and besides the purchase of the houses mentioned, he undertook to build the transepts and choir of the church, for which the space could now be left free. But in 1586, before the work could be begun, the Cardinal died, leaving the Congregation a legacy of 8000 crowns. His total benefactions had amounted to something like 20,000 crowns, and in 1588 the work on the transepts was taken in hand, so that by 1590 the whole structure of the church was complete. In the course of the next year Angelo Cesi, Bishop of Todi, and brother of Cardinal Pierdonato, came forward with an offer to build the façade of the church. He had already undertaken the decoration of the chapel in the left transept, as various friends of Philip and the Congregation had done in the case of other chapels ; while Cardinal Federigo Borromeo, the cousin of St Charles, built the high altar, though this was after Philip's death. It was not till 1606, eleven years after his death, that the façade was completed, and the finishing touch thus given to the Chiesa Nuova, the ' new church,' as it is still called.

Parallel with the construction of the church the work went on of moulding the Congregation into a definite form, and of drawing up its constitutions, as had been authorized in the bull of foundation. But in this matter the process was slower, and it was not until 1612, in the pontificate of Paul V, and seventeen years after Philip's death, that the constitutions in their final form received the approval of the Apostolic See.

The phrase, however, in the Bull of Gregory XIII of 1575, erecting in the church of S. Maria in Vallicella, ' a Congregation of secular priests and clerics,' enshrines the first essential point in Philip's mind, and one on which he always stood firm. The Clerks Regular, such as the Theatines and Barnabites, had already originated a new form of religious life in the church ; the Jesuits had introduced what was looked upon as a startling innovation, in that they were a religious order which was yet not bound to recite the Office in choir, as all the older orders did. Philip struck out a fresh line in founding an institute which should have rules, community life and a superior, but should not be a religious order at all.

Not that a community without vows was altogether unknown in Rome ; Philip himself was on very friendly terms with the community at the convent known as the Tor de' Specchi, founded by St Frances of Rome in 1433, and often went there to hear their confessions. The inhabitants of this convent are not, strictly speaking, nuns at all, but oblates, living together, and engaging in good works, under a superioress termed ' Presidente,' and under the spiritual care of the Olivetan monks at S. Maria Nuova (commonly called S. Francesca Romana) in the Forum ; and it has been suggested that Philip got the idea for his own Congregation from this community. At any rate, he thought there were religious orders enough already to suit every type of vocation, and he was determined not to found another one. And although there were influential members of the community who wished to introduce practices like those of religious—notably Fr. Antonio Talpa, who later succeeded in introducing in the Naples house an observance scarcely distinguishable from that of a religious order—Philip, who in other matters was always ready to defer to the views of others, would never consent to anything which tended to alter the status of the members of his Congregation from that of secular priests, bound to it by neither vow, oath nor promise.

An instance of this was his attitude—himself so strict in the practice of poverty—towards the possession of private property. In one draft of the constitutions it was proposed that the postulant, on entering the Congregation, should renounce his property ; but at this point (the document is still preserved) there is a marginal note in Philip's own handwriting : ' Habeat, retineat, sed videat ne qua sit lis ' (Let him have and keep it, but let him see that there is no litigation). But while the members of the Congregation retained the ownership of any property they might possess, those who could do so were expected not only to live on their own means, but also to contribute from them towards the general expenses of the house.

Philip's insistence on this principle led to a severe trial for Baronius. For Baronius, as we have seen, had no means of his own, and consequently had never contributed anything towards the upkeep of the house. But in 1586 Sixtus V assigned him a pension of 400 crowns for the purpose of printing his *Annals*, whereupon Philip at once told him that he must in future contribute towards the expenses of the house, as others did. This placed Baronius in a quandary : on the one hand it was a matter of conscience with him not to apply the money he received from the Pope to any purpose other than that for which it was given him, on the other Philip appeared adamant, and Baronius almost came to the resolution of leaving the Congregation. Eventually, on the advice of Fr. Tommaso Bozio, who had acted as his advocate, Baronius went and told Philip that he submitted absolutely, and would do as he wished. But now Philip relented, and told Baronius that no contribution would be demanded of him.

So essential was the exclusion of every kind of vow or oath ultimately realised to be to Philip's idea of the Congregation, that in the constitutions as finally approved in 1612 there appears a clause to the effect that, if in time to come even a majority of the Congregation should wish to introduce the taking of vows, those so wishing would be free to enter any religious order they might choose, but the minority, however small, so long as it remains faithful to the original status, is to be adjudged the true Congregation, with the right to all the Congregation's property.

But apart from his determination not to bind his Congregation by the vows of religion, Philip was averse from the idea of its eventually becoming a widespread body like a religious order, with a number of houses in different places under a central government. Again in this case there were many in the Congregation who saw in it the means of ultimately providing good and well-trained priests for bishops in all parts of Europe who needed them, and thus of forwarding the work of reformation in the Church. And if this was not the idea of its founder, it is not because he was not interested in wider issues. It would be absurd to impute to Philip a narrow or ' parochial ' outlook. His whole life is a proof that his spirit was as truly catholic in its breadth as it was apostolic in its zeal, from his youth, when he wished to go as a missionary to the Indies, to his extreme old age, when he intervened for the only time, so far as we know, in affairs of high ecclesiastical policy. This was the occasion in 1594 when he was induced to make use of his influence with Clement VIII, who had chosen Baronius as his confessor, to obtain the absolution of Henry of Navarre, simply because he was convinced of its vital importance for the welfare of the Church in France, and so of Catholicism in Europe.

The truth seems to be quite simply that he was not persuaded that he had the vocation to initiate any far-reaching work. God led certain men to him, and gave him an enormous influence over them ; that influence he would use to the full to make them love God, and serve the Church of Christ according to their several states and varying capabilities. That those whom he could thus influence would in their turn influence others, and thus—especially if they held high positions in the Church—help on the work of reform, he must have known, and would rejoice that it should be so. That the change in the religious spirit of Rome between the opening and the closing years of the sixteenth century is largely attributable to Philip personally is universally recognized. But that does not mean that the benefiting of the Church, as a whole was the end he explicitly set before himself as he devoted so much affectionate care to the souls of his individual penitents and friends.

In the case of the priests of his Congregation he wished that they should say Mass daily, practise mental prayer regularly, carry out the sacred functions with care and solemnity—in his own phrase, ' that they should have all the virtues of religious without their vows.' If they thus exemplified the highest ideals of the priesthood without departing from the status of secular priests, they might have an indirect effect on the rest of the secular clergy ; but it was not Philip's intention that his Congregation should be an instrument in their reform, or even in their formation. In fact, the constitutions he inspired explicitly preclude the direction of seminaries ; and it was when he fully understood Philip's conception of his own particular work that St Charles Borromeo finally gave up his attempts to establish the Oratory in Milan.

For from the earliest years St Charles had been anxious that Philip should send some of the fathers to his cathedral city—he was particularly anxious to have Tarugi there. After many delays four fathers were at length sent to Milan in 1575, but Tarugi was not amongst them, because he could not be spared from Rome, and in the next year they were all suddenly recalled. Negotiations for a foundation in Milan were continued for a time, but when St Charles fully understood that, even if they came, they would confine themselves to their own particular work, and not become subjects of his diocese whom he could employ as he pleased, he gave up the plan, and ultimately founded his Oblates of St Ambrose, now known as the Oblates of St Charles.

On the ground that the Roman house could not spare subjects, between 1570 and 1580 requests for foundations coming from Genoa, Bologna, Rimini, Ancona and Fermo were refused ; and although in 1579 three priests at San Severino were declared aggregated to the Congregation, no father was sent there from Rome.

If in 1586 another house was actually established at Naples, this was due primarily to Tarugi, who had gone there two years previously for his health, and had captivated the Neapolitans by his sermons given in the cathedral in the informal manner of the Oratory. He was soon as anxious himself to be allowed to make a foundation in Naples as the Neapolitans were to have him, and he succeeded, though a good deal of persuasion was necessary, in obtaining Philip's consent to the project. Besides Tarugi, Fathers Talpa and Giovenale Ancina were sent to Naples with one or two others, and the foundation flourished. But the government of another house at a distance was a great anxiety and burden to Philip, who from 1576 onwards was often ill, and missed Tarugi badly. His burden was greatly increased when the gift, by a benefactor, of an abbey in the Abbruzzi, intended to help them financially, gave him the responsibility of having practically episcopal jurisdiction over a number of distant parishes.

The government of Naples by Rome lasted only until 1602, San Severino having been given up in the preceding year. Since then it has always been regarded as a cardinal principle of the Oratory that each Congregation is entirely self-governing and independent of all others, a principle explicitly laid down in the constitutions.

As regards the internal government of the Congregation, though Philip himself was elected superior for life, the constitutions lay it down that this office lasts for three years only, though the same one may be re-elected. He is assisted by four ' deputies,' also elected for three years. Philip personally would never allow himself to be given any title indicating his superiorship other than that of ' Father ' ; and when St Charles once asked him how it was that he was so perfectly obeyed, his answer was, ' Because I command little.' For this reason, though the constitutions speak of the ' Præpositus '—in English ' Provost '—and he is so termed in official documents, in the ordinary way the superior of an Oratory is spoken of by the community simply as ' the Father.' A notable feature of the constitutions is that they take the form rather of a record of established customs than of a series of precepts : they say not so much that this or that *must be done* as that all priests of the Congregation *do* say Mass daily, or whatever it may be.

Since the end of the institute is summed up as being prayer, preaching and the administration of the sacraments, the constitutions speak of daily sermons, which are to be simple and familiar, avoiding intricate questions and discussions, and lay it down that the fathers must be constantly in the confessional—at certain times all, and one at least every day—while the principal community exercise every day is the half-hour of mental prayer at the evening ' Oratory ' already described. On feasts there is to be a solemn High Mass, and the community assists in choir at Vespers. One quite peculiar observance is in connection with the refectory, where, after the reading customary in all religious houses, two ' doubts,' as they are called (that is, debatable questions), are proposed, one a point of moral theology, the other from Scripture ; each speaks in turn on one of these, the proposer finally summing up, and giving a solution of the ' doubt.' This custom dates from the very first establishment of Philip's disciples at S. Giovanni de' Fiorentini, and the few rules he drew up to regulate their daily life there.

NOTE.—With the promulgation of the new Code of Canon Law in 1918 the obligation was imposed on all religious orders and institutes of revising their constitutions in such points as might be necessary in order to bring them into conformity with the prescriptions of the new Code. In September 1933 representatives of the various Congregations of the Oratory met in Rome to decide upon the revisions thus rendered necessary in the case of the constitutions of the Oratory. The revised constitutions have not yet been issued, but it may be stated that such changes as have been proposed are only in the direction of defining more explicitly the object of the institute, and of adapting certain points to suit the changed conditions of our times, the basic principles explained in this chapter remaining entirely unaltered.

XII

THE year 1583 is notable in Philip's life for a
remarkable miracle, well attested by eye-
witnesses. This was the raising to life of Paolo de'
Massimi, the son of Fabrizio de' Massimi, whose
name occurs so frequently amongst Philip's friends—
the same who used to find it enough to stand near
the door of Philip's room to cure a fit of depression.
Philip had foretold that this child would be a boy
when Fabrizio's wife had borne him five daughters
in succession, and he had been allowed to choose a
name for him.

Early in January 1583, when he was fourteen
years old, Paolo became ill with fever, which
continued without abatement till March. By the
middle of the month he was clearly near the point of
death, and Philip, who had been visiting him daily,
wished to be sent for when the end approached.
On March 16 an urgent message was sent for him to
come at once, but Philip was just then saying Mass,
and by the time he arrived at the house, half an
hour later, Paolo was dead, and the body was
already being prepared for burial. Fabrizio met
Philip on the stairs and led him to the room. There
he prayed at the side of the bed for seven or eight
minutes, with his usual trembling and palpitation
of the heart ; then rising, he sprinkled the boy with
holy water, putting a little in his mouth, breathed

on him, and laid his hands on his forehead, and then called him twice by name, ' Paolo, Paolo ! ' whereupon the boy opened his eyes and began to talk. He talked with Philip for a quarter of an hour, and gave other clear signs of life. At the end of that time Philip asked him if he would now be willing to die, and go to see his mother and sister in Heaven. Paolo replied in a clear voice that he was quite willing, and with Philip's blessing died again.

Fabrizio, with his second wife, Paolo's stepmother, and a maid were all eye-witnesses of the scene, and there was no kind of doubt in the mind of any of them either of Paolo's having really died, or of his having been really alive again. The room in the Palazzo Massimi where this happened was turned into a chapel, and the sixteenth of March is still celebrated there as the ' feast of the miracle ' with a special Mass.

In 1585 Gregory XIII, the great benefactor of the Oratory, and the first to give the Congregation formal recognition, died. He was succeeded by the Franciscan friar, Felice Perretti, who took the name of Sixtus V—a stern and rigorous ruler, and a great builder. And if Philip was not on terms of familiar friendship with this pontiff in the way that he had been in the preceding pontificate, and would be in still greater degree under succeeding Popes, he was by now looked upon with veneration by nearly all the members of the Sacred College, many of whom were visitors to his room, while not a few were his penitents and avowedly his disciples. It would not be of particular interest to give the whole list of cardinals who visited him, but some of those in the category of his intimate friends must be mentioned.

The name of Agostino Valiero, the Cardinal of Verona, has already occurred as the author of the dialogue which he called ' Philip, or Christian Joy.' Equally devoted to Philip was the Cardinal of Bologna, Gabriele Paleotto, who also wrote a book, *De Bono Senectutis*, which was published with Philip's portrait as a frontispiece, and held him up as an example of all that is beautiful in old age. It was at Paleotto's prompting that Cardinal Pierdonato Cesi had become such a munificent benefactor of the Congregation.

Cardinals Cusano and Federigo Borromeo chose Philip for their confessor, and used to go to visit him every day. The latter had been asked for by the Milanese as their archbishop, in succession to St Charles, his cousin. By nature fond of retirement and study, he was pious and scrupulous, and so was unwilling to accept so heavy a responsibility ; it was only Philip's advice, whom he consulted in everything, that eventually made him decide to accept it. It was these two Cardinals, with Cardinal Montalto, who were privileged to send Philip every day two small loaves, some eggs and a little bottle of wine, because it pleased him to live like a poor man entirely on what he received as alms.

Cardinal Cusano was able in 1590, the last year of the pontificate of Sixtus V, to give Philip a great joy. For he obtained permission to have translated to the Vallicella the bodies of the martyrs SS. Papias and Maurus, which had been discovered, together with those of other martyrs, in the course of building operations in his titular church of S. Adriano in the Forum. The relics were taken in solemn procession, on February 11, from S. Adriano to the Vallicella, where ten Cardinals, as well as Philip and the whole community, were assembled to meet them. They were exposed on an altar in the church for four days, and were then taken to the sacristy to await the consecration of the church. When this took place, in 1599, the heads of the martyrs were enshrined in silver reliquaries, and the bodies were placed under the high altar.

Philip seized the opportunity provided by the solemn translation of the relics to the Vallicella for an attempt to draw public ridicule upon himself. In full view of the crowd gathered at the church to await the arrival of the procession with the relics, he went up to one of the Swiss Guards on duty at the door, and began pulling and stroking his beard.

Another Cardinal who was on affectionate terms with Philip, and was a frequent visitor at the Vallicella when he was in Rome, was Nicolò Sfondrato, Bishop of Cremona. And not only did Philip once make him try on the beretta of Pius V to see how it would suit him, but one day after the death of Sixtus V, in 1590, when the Cardinal of Cremona was announced at the Vallicella, Philip commanded those present to kneel down and kiss his feet. This prophecy seemed to be falsified by the election shortly afterwards of Cardinal Castagna, who took the name of Urban VII. This pontificate, however, lasted only twelve days, and in the conclave that followed it Cardinal Sfondrato was elected Pope, and became Gregory XIV.

When Philip presented himself to offer his homage, the new Pope, after embracing him affectionately, placed on his head the red beretta that he had worn himself, saying, 'We create you Cardinal.' That it was meant seriously was shown by the fact that the

Pope at the same time gave directions for the necessary brief to be prepared, but by a few whispered words Philip prevailed on the Pope to allow him to treat the matter as no more than a joke. Afterwards he used jokingly to twit the Secretary with the long delay in making out his brief, and ask him when it was going to be ready. Renewed pressure on the part of the Pope was met with the reply that he was deeply grateful, and would let His Holiness know when he was ready to accept the cardinalate. At the same time, whenever he went to an audience, the Pope made him be seated and cover his head in his presence, like a member of the Sacred College.

One favour he did accept from Gregory XIV. This was the privilege obtained for him by Cardinal Cusano of saying Mass in a private chapel near his room, so that he no longer needed to exert himself to restrain his ecstasies, as he did when he celebrated in public. His extraordinary Masses in this little chapel have been described by his earliest biographers. When he came to the Agnus Dei the server lighted a little lamp, put out the altar candles and closed the shutters ; then he withdrew with anyone else who was present at the Mass. The door was locked, and on it a little card was hung to say, ' Silence ! The Father is saying Mass.' In two hours or so the server returned and knocked at the door. If Philip answered he entered and the Mass was resumed. If there was no answer he went away again and returned later, though even then Philip complained that the time was too short.

Equally striking was the devotion he showed when he received the Blessed Sacrament in bed during his illnesses. Once, in the year 1577, because he had had no sleep Tarugi gave directions that he should not be given Communion, for fear that his fervour would take away any chance of his getting to sleep, but Philip sent for him and said : ' Francesco Maria, I tell you that I cannot sleep for the desire I have of the Blessed Sacrament ; make them bring me Communion and I shall go to sleep directly I have received it.' He showed the same kind of agitation another night even because Fr. Antonio Gallonio was somehow slow in giving him the Host. ' Antonio,' he said, ' why do you hold my Lord in your hand, and not give Him to me ? '

Shortly after the election of Gregory XIV Philip fell seriously ill, and though by the end of the year he had recovered, he was in weak health, and often definitely ill, for the remainder of his life. In the following year, 1591, he had the sorrow of losing Fr. Nicolò Gigli, a Frenchman, and one of his earliest disciples, whom he loved for his humility and his unwearyingly devoted life. He held for many years the position of confessor to the nuns at the Tor de' Specchi. But in accordance with his own saying that ' in this life God always sends us first a cross and then a consolation,' the year which saw the death of Gigli saw also the entrance into the Congregation of Pietro Consolini. In his case Philip took the extraordinary step of proposing him to the fathers, and having him admitted to the Congregation, without even telling the young man what he was doing. And for the rest of Philip's life, though without displacing the faithful Germanico Fedeli and Antonio Gallonio, Pietro was in constant attendance on the old man, whether giving him his arm when he went out, or reciting the Office with him in his room. In return Philip opened out more fully to the young novice than to anyone else ;

it was Pietro, for example, who shared with
Cardinal Federigo Borromeo alone the privilege of
hearing from Philip's own lips the story of his experience in the catacombs of S. Sebastiano, when
the globe of fire appeared and his heart was
miraculously enlarged.

But Pietro's training included its due measure of
mortification. One day when he was preparing a
sermon he was told that he must compose instead
a kind of comic almanack, to be ready by the
evening : nor was the protest made to Philip by the
father who was prefect of preachers of any avail.
In the evening the almanack had to be read aloud
before several Cardinals, who were so much amused
that they bore it off to show it to the Pope. And
what must the poor young man's feeling have been
as he faithfully obeyed Philip's injunction, on an
occasion when he had to undergo an examination
before the Pope, to tell the examiners that he was a
man of education, and that there was no need to
examine such as he. There is no record of what the
examiners thought, but the Pope himself knew
Philip too well to misunderstand.

In October 1591 Gregory XIV died, having been
Pope only just ten months, to the sorrow of Philip
and his community. But following the pontificate
of Innocent IX, who lived only two months after
his election, there succeeded to the papal throne a
Cardinal who had been a friend and admirer of
Philip's for thirty years, Ippolito Aldobrandini,
who became Clement VIII.

The accession of Clement VIII brings us to the
closing years of Philip's life. He had been born
when Leo X was Pope, and, as Capecelatro points
out, a comparison between the reign of Leo X—

brilliant, but worldly and even profane—and that of Clement VIII, which was wholly in keeping with the character of a Pope who was personally devout and austere, hard-working and zealous, gives us the measure of the advance the Church had made in the way of reform during the sixteenth century, an advance which Philip had done so much to further.

Clement would have wished Philip to be his confessor now that he was Pope as he had been before, but his age and illnesses made quite impossible the frequent going and coming between the Vatican and the Vallicella which this would have involved, and so in 1594 the Pope chose Baronius in his place. But Philip frequently went to visit him and was always received with the greatest affection.

On one such visit paid only two months before his own death, Philip found the Pope suffering badly from gout. So acute was the pain that he could not bear anyone to touch even his bed, and as soon as Philip came forward he told him not to come any nearer. Philip, however, took no notice, but advancing to the side of the bed said, ' Your Holiness need have no fear,' and with these words he caught hold of the Pope's hand and pressed it firmly and affectionately, trembling in his usual way. As he did so the pain ceased. The Pope often afterwards related this occurrence as a miracle, and a proof of Philip's sanctity.

The kind of terms that Philip could employ with the Pope are best shown by a letter he addressed to Clement VIII, which is still preserved, and the Pope's reply written on the same sheet. After telling him that many of the Cardinals had been to see him, and that seven hours after nightfall

Jesus himself had come to abide with him, whereas he (the Pope) had never once been to visit their church, he goes on : ' I command Your Holiness to do my bidding in the matter of a girl I wish to put into the Tor de' Specchi ; she is the daughter of Claudio Neri, whose children you have promised to care for, and I must remind you that it befits a Pope to keep his promises. Wherefore let Your Holiness put this matter into my hands, so that I may use your name in case of need ; the more so that I know the mind of the girl, and am sure she is moved by an inspiration from God. And with all befitting humility I kiss the feet of Your Holiness.'

Clement replied in the same vein : ' The Pope says that the first part of your petition breathes somewhat of an ambitious spirit, in that you tell him cardinals visit you so often ; unless, indeed, you wish to let him know that these are spiritual men, which he knows well enough already. As to his going to see you, he says that Your Reverence does not deserve it, since you will not accept the cardinalate so many times offered you. In regard to the command, he allows you to scold those good mothers with your wonted severity if they will not do what you wish ; and in his turn he commands you to take care of yourself, and not to go back to the confessional without his leave ; and that when next Our Lord comes to you, you pray for him and for the pressing needs of Christendom.'

This reply shows that Clement VIII, too, wished to make Philip a Cardinal, but now his age and infirmities provided him with an adequate excuse for declining it. If anyone spoke to him of accepting the purple he would raise his eyes—or even toss his beretta in the air—exclaiming, 'Paradiso! Paradiso!'

But if the Pope did not insist in Philip's own case, his pleas and protests did not succeed in preventing the Pope from taking other members from his Congregation. The first to go was Bordini, who, early in the pontificate, was appointed Bishop of Cavaillon, a suffragan see of Avignon. In October 1592 Tarugi was ordered to return from Naples to Rome, and to hold himself in readiness ; on November 15 he was told that he was to be made Archbishop of Avignon, nor could either Tarugi's own entreaties or Philip's induce the Pope to go back on his decision. And though no more subjects were taken from the Congregation in Philip's life-time, in the year following his death Baronius was made first Protonotary Apostolic, and a little later Cardinal. In the same consistory Tarugi was also made a Cardinal, and translated from Avignon to Siena. Finally, though this too was after Philip's death, Giovenale Ancina was made Bishop of Saluzzo, in the territory of the Duke of Savoy.

Towards the end of 1592 Philip was again so seriously ill that his doctor did not expect him to live. Philip himself, however, assured the doctor that he would not die of this illness, and that he would hear the confessions of his regular penitents at Christmas ; and this in fact he did.

It was probably this illness that finally comfirmed his resolution to obtain release from his position as Provost of the Congregation. An appeal to the fathers to let him resign having proved unsuccess-ful, he turned to Cardinals Cusano and Borromeo for help. They, therefore, went first to the Pope, and having obtained his consent assembled the fathers of the Congregation, and told them that it was the Pope's wish that they should grant Philip's request to be relieved of his burden, adding that he wished Baronius to succeed him as superior. The fathers could hardly refuse any longer, now that Philip's request was expressly supported by the Pope ; but Baronius at once protested that he could on no account consent to become superior unless there was a free election, held in accordance with their constitutions. Accordingly, there was an interval of three weeks, to enable the fathers at Naples to be consulted and, if they wished, to come and vote. At the end of this time the election was held, the absent fathers leaving everything in the hands of those in Rome, and resulted in the unanimous choice of Baronius.

In April 1594 Philip was very ill with fever, succeeded by an attack of gravel, and on the sixteenth, after many continuous hours of pain, he was so exhausted, and his pulse so weak, that the doctors pronounced that he could not now live long. The curtains of his bed were drawn, and the doctors with a few friends of Philip's, after talking for a short while in a corner of the room, had lapsed into silence. Suddenly they heard Philip saying in a loud voice : ' He who desires ought else but God deceives himself utterly. Ah, my most holy Madonna, my beautiful Madonna, my blessed Madonna ! ' Pulling back the curtains they saw Philip with his hands lifted, and his body raised in the air about a foot above the bed, stretching out his arms as though embracing someone with great affection. He remained like this for some while, invoking Our Lady and weeping, though no one else could see anything, till one of the doctors asked him what was the matter. Again lying on his bed he answered, ' Did you not see the Madonna who came to free

me from my pain ? ' Then, as though suddenly
coming to himself, he looked round, and, seeing
so many people present, he covered his face with
the sheet and burst into tears.

When he was calm again he said to the doctors,
' I have no need of your services any longer ; the
Madonna has come and healed me.' After they
had taken his pulse and examined him they were
satisfied that the fever was gone, and he was so
much better that next day he even got up. When
Cardinals Cusano and Borromeo heard what had
happened they at once came to see Philip, and
prevailed on him to tell them all about the vision,
and they in their turn told the Pope. All the rest
of that evening, we are told, Philip did nothing but
recommend devotion to Our Lady as the great
means of obtaining graces from God.

XIII

PHILIP'S LAST YEARS AND DEATH

FOR nearly a year afterwards Philip's health seems to have been fairly good, and it was during this time that he gave active support to the cause of the Duke of Nevers, the Ambassador of Henry of Navarre. The King had already made his abjuration of the Calvinist heresy before the Archbishop of Bourges, who had conditionally absolved him, but as he was a relapsed heretic his definitive absolution was reserved to the Pope. Philip used all his influence with the Pope to obtain the King's absolution, because he was convinced that it would be for the good of the Church in France, and this in spite of the fact that the Spanish party in Rome, which was strongly opposed to the granting of the absolution, included his friends Cardinals Cusano and Borromeo. He even made Baronius threaten to refuse to act as confessor to the Pope any longer unless he absolved the King of Navarre.

On March 30, 1595, another attack of fever came on, and the next day he sent for Fr. Flaminio Ricci, who was at Naples, that he might see him before he died. Tarugi at Avignon was too far off to be summoned, and Philip never saw him again after he left Rome. Fr. Ricci wrote back to say that he could not leave Naples till September, nor could three more letters make him understand that it was urgent that he should come at once. As a fourth

was despatched Philip murmured that now it
would be too late.

The fever lasted almost the whole of April, but
he was able to say Mass, as he had specially hoped
and prayed to do, for his own feast, SS. Philip and
James, on May 1. For the next three days he did
not say Mass, in obedience to his doctor's orders, but
he said it again daily up till May 12. That day there
was a serious hæmorrhage from his lungs—so
serious that, though it was impossible to give him
Viaticum, Baronius anointed him, in the presence
of Cardinal Borromeo. When the hæmorrhage
stopped the Cardinal asked to be allowed to give
him Holy Viaticum himself. As the Blessed Sacrament was borne into the room Philip opened his
eyes, and made many fervent ejaculations. He said
the Domine non sum dignus with the Cardinal, and
added, ' I never was worthy, for I have never done
any good.'

' Now I have received the true Physician of my
soul,' he said, when he had been given Communion.

In the evening there was a return of the hæmorrhage, with a violent cough and some difficulty
in breathing. Noticing the look of alarm on the
face of one of those present Philip said, ' Are you
afraid ? I have not the least fear.' The next morning, however, the doctors found him free from pain
and much better ; and he told them it was due to
remedies more efficacious than theirs—the Masses
and prayers said for him in a number of religious
houses to which he had sent alms. From that day
till the 26th, when he died, he was able to say Mass
and his Office every day, and also to hear confessions. But on the 24th there was a significant incident : Philip collected all his letters and papers,

everything he had ever written that he could lay
his hands on, and burned them.

Bacci's account of Philip's last hours and of his
death is consecrated by tradition. No apology,
therefore, is needed for reproducing it almost
verbally.

The feast of Corpus Christi in 1595 fell on May 25,
and Philip gave orders that all who wanted to come
to confession were to be admitted. He began hearing confessions very early in the morning, as though
he were in perfect health. He asked many of his
penitents to say a rosary for him after his death, and
gave it to some as a penance : he gave them all
special instructions, enjoining on them particularly
the frequentation of the sacraments, hearing sermons
and reading the lives of the Saints, and to all he
showed even more than his usual affection.

The confessions being ended he said the canonical
hours with great devotion, and then said Mass in his
little chapel two hours earlier than usual. At the
beginning of his Mass he remained for some time
looking towards S. Onofrio, on the slope of the
Janiculum, which was visible from the chapel. On
coming to the Gloria he began to sing, and sang
it all through ; all the rest of the Mass he said with
extraordinary joy and exultation. After Mass he
gave Communion to several persons. When he had
made his thanksgiving a little soup was brought to
him, and he murmured, ' They think that I am
recovered, but it is not so ' ; afterwards he went
back again to the confessional.

Cardinals Cusano and Borromeo came in to see
him on their way back from the procession of the
Blessed Sacrament, and stayed talking to him till
dinner time. As soon as the Cardinals had left

him he had his usual slight meal, and after a short
rest said Vespers and Compline. The rest of the day
he spent partly in conversation with those who came
to see him, and partly in having the Lives of the
Saints read to him, particularly that of St Bernadine
of Siena, which he had read over to him a second
time.

At five o'clock Cardinal Cusano came a second
time with Girolamo Pamfili, an auditor of the Rota,
and soon afterwards the Bishop of Montepulciano.
With these visitors Philip said the Matins of the
next day's Office, ' the rest of which,' Bacci says,
' he was to finish with the angels and saints in
Paradise.' Having finished Matins they left the
place where they had said Office, and on Cardinal
Cusano's offering to help Philip up a staircase, he
refused with a smile saying, ' Do you think I have
not got quite strong again ? ' A little later his
doctor came in, not as a doctor, he said, but as a
friend ; but he felt his pulse and said, ' Why,
Father, you are better than ever before ; for these
last ten years I have never seen you in such excellent
health.' Philip afterwards heard the Cardinal's
confession, and when he left went with him to the
top of the stairs, looking intently at him and
pressing his hands, to say good-bye.

During the rest of the day down to supper time
he heard several more confessions. He had his
supper alone, as usual, and after supper heard the
confessions of the fathers who were to say the first
Masses next day. After this many of the community
came, according to custom, to get his blessing.

At the third hour of the night (that is, about
eleven o'clock) he said his usual prayers and went
to bed, apparently perfectly well, but as soon as he

was in bed he said once more, with great earnestness,
the words which he so often repeated : ' Last of all
we must die.' Shortly afterwards he asked the time,
and on being told that three had just struck he said,
as if to himself, ' Three and two are five, three and
three are six, and then I shall go.' He then lay
down in bed and dismissed all who were with
him.

When it had struck five (one o'clock in the morning, that is) he got up and began walking up and
down his room, whereupon Fr. Antonio Gallonio,
who slept in the room below, ran up and found him
lying on his bed with a violent cough, and with
blood pouring from his mouth. Gallonio asked
him how he felt, and he replied : ' Antonio,
I am going.' Gallonio then ran for help and sent
for the doctor. When he returned Philip was sitting
on his bed, and in this position he remained till he
died. They did what they could for him, and
succeeded in stopping the cough, so that in a quarter
of an hour he could speak distinctly and seemed to
have recovered, but he said to them : ' Do not
trouble yourselves to apply remedies, for I am
dying.'

In the meanwhile all the fathers had been called
to his room, and knelt around his bed while Baronius, as superior, made the commendation of his
soul. When it was ended the doctor felt his pulse
and told the fathers he was dying, which they had
scarcely realised because he was sitting up, and only
appeared to have some difficulty in breathing. On
this Baronius at once asked him in a loud voice,
' Father, are you going to leave us without saying a
word to us ? At least give us your blessing.' At
these words Philip lifted his hand slightly, and

opening his eyes, which till then had been closed, raised them towards heaven and kept them fixed there for some time ; then lowering them towards the fathers who were kneeling round he made a gentle inclination of the head towards them, as if he had obtained for them the blessing of God, and thus, without another word, but as if gently falling asleep, he died.

Before the doors were opened in the morning, the body was clothed in priest's vestments and carried down by the whole community into the church. As soon as the news of his death spread through Rome throngs of people of all sorts and conditions began to arrive, and flowers that the fathers placed on the corpse were taken away at once as relics. Later in the morning the Office of the Dead was recited and a solemn Mass of Requiem sung. All day long the crowds continued ; but after the church was closed in the evening the physicians and surgeons who had known him proceeded to open the body, to investigate the mysterious swelling on his breast. Examination proved that the two ribs over the heart were broken and arched outwards ; the heart was unusually large, while the great artery leading from it was twice the normal size ; there was no sign of any disease. At the same time the præcordia were extracted, and a plaster cast was taken of his face.

After this the body was taken back to the church, and remained exposed the whole of the next day. In the evening it was placed in an ordinary coffin, and the fathers wished to leave it in the common burying-place of the Congregation beneath the choir of the church. Cardinals Borromeo and de' Medici, however, intervened, and the body was eventually laid in a walnut coffin, which was placed in a space above the first arch of the nave of the church.

Among the many who came to pray at Philip's tomb was a certain Nero del Nero, who had been most devoted to Philip during his life, and before long he decided to provide a rich silver coffin for the body. As a preparatory step, on March 9, 1599, the coffin was brought down and opened, and although a large amount of dust had got in, and the vestments had all completely decayed, the body itself was found to be in an almost perfect state of preservation. On May 13, the body, newly vested in the chasuble he had worn at his last Mass, was transferred to a new coffin of cypress wood lined with red silk, and was temporarily replaced above the arch of the nave.

For now Nero del Nero had resolved not merely to provide a new coffin, but to build a chapel as a token of his devotion, and in thanksgiving for the birth of an heir, which he attributed to Philip's intercession. In July 1600 the first stone was laid by Tarugi, now a Cardinal, and on May 24, 1602, the body, borne by the six oldest fathers, was translated into the rich and beautiful chapel which is now the Saint's shrine. In 1639 the coffin was once more opened for relics to be extracted, but afterwards it was placed in a wrought-iron case covered with silver, and so remained till recent years. But in 1922, the year of the third centenary of Philip's canonization, this iron case was opened and the body, newly vested, was placed in a crystal urn, to be carried in triumph through the streets of Rome—the first procession of the kind since 1870— and then replaced once more beneath the altar of the chapel, where it can now be exposed to the veneration of the faithful.

While Philip was still alive Clement VIII himself was amongst those who said that he would one day certainly be canonized, and after his death he was proclaimed on all sides to be a Saint. From the day of his death there were reports of visions of him in glory seen by various nuns and holy persons, and of miracles obtained by touching his body or by invoking his prayers. But official processes move more slowly, and although the first was begun as early as August 2, 1595, only two months after his death, it was Paul V who decreed his beatification on May 25, 1615. This same Pope also formally approved the constitutions of the Congregation of the Oratory.

On March 12, 1622, the jealous citizens of Rome were saying that that morning in S. Peter's the Pope—it was Gregory XV—had canonized ' four Spaniards and a Saint ! ' The ' Spaniards ' were Isidore the farmer of Madrid, Ignatius of Loyola, Francis Xavier and Teresa of Avila—no less. The ' Saint,' of course, was Rome's second Apostle, Philip Neri.

INDEX

CONGREGATIONS OF THE ORATORY IN 1984

Italy and Sicily
Acireale
Biella
Bologna
Brescia
Cava dei Tirreni
Chioggia
Florence
Genoa
Guardia Sanframondi
Mondovi
Naples
Palermo
Perugia
Rome
Turin
Vicenza
Verona

Spain
Albacete
Alcala de Henares
Barcelona
Gracia (Barcelona)
Palma (Mallorca)
Porreras (Mallorca)
Seville
Soller (Mallorca)
Tudela
Vich

Germany (West)
Aachen
Frankfurt-am-Main
Heidelberg
Munich

Germany (East)
Dresden
Frankfurt-Oder
Leipzig

Austria
Vienna

Switzerland
Zurich

Poland
Bytow
Gostyn
Radom
Studzianna
Tarnow
Tomaszow

U.S.A.
Monterey, CA
Pharr, TX
Pittsburgh, PA
Rock Hill, SC

England
Birmingham
London

Mexico
Guanajuato
Leon
Mexico City
Orizaba
Puebla
San Miguel de Allende
San Pablo Tepetlapa (Mexico City)
Tlalnepantla (Mexico City)

Canada
Toronto

Colombia
Bogota
Ipiales
Pasto

Costa Rica
San Jose

Chile
Villa Alemana

OTHER TITLES AVAILABLE

The Glories of Mary. St. Alphonsus.
The Prophets and Our Times. Culleton.
St. Therese, The Little Flower. Beevers.
The Life & Glories of St. Joseph. Thompson.
An Explanation of the Baltimore Catechism. Kinkead.
Humility of Heart. da Bergamo.
Christ's Appeal for Love. Menendez.
The Cure D'Ars. Trochu.
The Divine Mysteries of the Rosary. Ven. M. of Agreda.
Preparation for Death. St. Alphonsus.
St. Joseph of Copertino. Pastrovicchi.
Mary, The Second Eve. Card. Newman.
The Faith of Our Fathers. Gibbons.
Manual of Practical Devotion to St. Joseph. Patrignani.
The Wonder of Guadalupe. Johnston.
The Blessed Virgin Mary. St. Alphonsus.
The Way of Divine Love. Menendez.
St. Pius V. Anderson.
Mystical City of God—Abridged. Ven. M. of Agreda.
Beyond Space—A Book About the Angels. Parente.
Dialogue of St. Catherine of Siena. Thorold.
Evidence of Satan in the Modern World. Cristiani.
Child's Bible History. Knecht.
Bible History of the Old & New Testaments. Schuster.
Apologetics. Glenn.
Magnificent Prayers. St. Bridget of Sweden.
Baltimore Catechism No. 3. Kinkead.
The Blessed Eucharist. Mueller.
Soul of the Apostolate. Chautard.
Thirty Favorite Novenas.
Devotion to the Infant Jesus of Prague.
Fundamentals of Catholic Dogma. Ott.
The Agony of Jesus. Padre Pio.
Uniformity with God's Will. St. Alphonsus.
St. Gertrude the Great.
St. Joan of Arc. Beevers.
Life of the Blessed Virgin Mary. Emmerich.
Convert's Catechism of Catholic Doctrine. Geiermann.
Canons & Decrees of the Council of Trent. Schroeder.

At your bookdealer or direct from the Publisher.

OTHER TITLES AVAILABLE

Trustful Surrender to Divine Providence.
The Sinner's Return to God. Mueller.
A Year with the Saints.
Saint Michael and the Angels.
The Dolorous Passion of Our Lord. Emmerich.
Modern Saints—Their Lives & Faces. Ball.
Our Lady of Fatima's Peace Plan from Heaven.
Divine Favors Granted to St. Joseph. Binet.
St. Joseph Cafasso—Priest of the Gallows. St. John Bosco.
Catechism of the Council of Trent.
The Foot of the Cross. Fr. Faber.
The Rosary in Action. Johnson.
Padre Pio—The Stigmatist. Carty.
The Life of Anne Catherine Emmerich. 2 Vols. Schmoger.
Fatima—The Great Sign. Johnston.
Wife, Mother and Mystic. Bessieres.
St. Rose of Lima. Sister Alphonsus.
Charity for the Suffering Souls. Nageleisen.
Devotion to the Sacred Heart of Jesus. Verheylezoon.
Who Is Padre Pio?
The Stigmata and Modern Science. Carty.
The Incorruptibles. Cruz.
The Life of Christ. 4 Vols. Emmerich.
St. Dominic. Dorcy.
Is It a Saint's Name? Dunne.
St. Anthony—The Wonder Worker of Padua. Stoddard.
The Precious Blood. Fr. Faber.
The Holy Shroud & Four Visions. O'Connell.
Clean Love in Courtship. Lovasik.
The Devil. Delaporte.
Too Busy for God? Think Again! D'Angelo.
The Prophecies of St. Malachy. Bander.
St. Martin de Porres. Cavallini.
The Secret of the Rosary. St. Louis De Montfort.
The History of Antichrist. Huchede.
The Douay-Rheims New Testament.
Purgatory Explained. Schouppe.
St. Catherine of Siena. Curtayne.
Where We Got the Bible. Graham.

At your bookdealer or direct from the Publisher.

Imitation of the Sacred Heart of Jesus. Arnoudt.
Alexandrina—The Agony & The Glory. Johnston.
Blessed Margaret of Castello. Bonniwell.
The Ways of Mental Prayer. Lehodey.
St. Dominic's Family. Dorcy.
Be My Son. Legere.
Sermons of St. Alphonsus Liguori.
The Catholic Answer to the Jehovah's Witnesses. D'Angelo.
What Faith Really Means. Graham.
A Catechism of Modernism. Lemius.
What Catholics Believe. Lovasik.
Spiritual Conferences. Tauler.
Treatise on the Love of God. St. Francis de Sales.
Purgatory and Heaven. Arendzen.
Conversation with Christ. Rohrbach.
Bethlehem. Faber.
Book of Infinite Love. de la Touche.
The Church Teaches. Jesuit Fathers.
Mary, Mother of the Church. Ripley.
Who Is Teresa Neumann? Carty.
The Priesthood. Stockums.
Evolution Hoax Exposed. Field.
Light and Peace. Quadrupani.
Marriage and the Family. Sheed.
Radio Replies. 3 Vol. Rumble & Carty.
Incarnation, Birth and Infancy of Jesus Christ. Liguori.
Passion and Death of Jesus Christ. Liguori.
Bible Quizzes. Rumble & Carty.
Meditation Prayer on Mary Immaculate. Padre Pio.
Why Squander Illness? Carty.
Story of the Church. Johnson, et al.
Creator and Creature. Faber.
Pere Lamy. Bivers.
The Primitive Church. Lanslots.
Mystical Evolution. Arintero.
The Priest, the Man of God. St. Joseph Cafasso.
New Regulations on Indulgences. Herbst.
True Church Quizzes. Rumble and Carty.
Three Ways of the Spiritual Life. Garrigou-Lagrange.

At your bookdealer or direct from the Publisher.

NOTES

NOTES

NOTES

NOTES